# MznLnx

*Missing Links Exam Preps*

Exam Prep for

## College Algrbra

### Beecher & Penna & Bittinger, 2nd Edition

The MznLnx Exam Prep is your link from the texbook and lecture to your exams.
The MznLnx Exam Preps are unauthorized and comprehensive reviews of your textbooks.

All material provided by MznLnx and Rico Publications (c) 2010
Textbook publishers and textbook authors do not particpate in or contribute to these reviews.

# MznLnx

Rico
Publications

*Exam Prep for College Algrbra*
2nd Edition
Beecher & Penna & Bittinger

*Publisher:* Raymond Houge
*Assistant Editor:* Michael Rouger
*Text and Cover Designer:* Lisa Buckner
*Marketing Manager:* Sara Swagger
*Project Manager, Editorial Production:* Jerry Emerson
*Art Director:* Vernon Lowerui

*Product Manager:* Dave Mason
*Editorial Assitant:* Rachel Guzmanji
*Pedagogy:* Debra Long
*Cover Image:* Jim Reed/Getty Images
*Text and Cover Printer:* City Printing, Inc.
*Compositor:* Media Mix, Inc.

(c) 2010 Rico Publications
ALL RIGHTS RESERVED. No part of this work
covered by the copyright may be reproduced or
used in any form or by an means--graphic, electronic,
or mechanical, including photocopying, recording,
taping, Web distribution, information storage, and
retrieval systems, or in any other manner--without the
written permission of the publisher.

For more information about our products, contact us at:
Dave.Mason@RicoPublications.com

For permission to use material from this text or
product, submit a request online to:
Dave.Mason@RicoPublications.com

Printed in the United States
ISBN:

# Contents

**CHAPTER 1**
*Graphs, Functions, and Models* — 1

**CHAPTER 2**
*Functions, Equations, and Inequalities* — 14

**CHAPTER 3**
*Polynomial and Rational Functions* — 34

**CHAPTER 4**
*Exponential and Logarithmic Functions* — 50

**CHAPTER 5**
*Systems of Equations and Matrices* — 68

**CHAPTER 6**
*Conic Sections* — 92

**CHAPTER 7**
*Sequences, Series, and Combinatorics* — 103

**ANSWER KEY** — 117

# TO THE STUDENT

### COMPREHENSIVE

The *MznLnx* Exam Prep series is designed to help you pass your exams. Editors at MznLnx review your textbooks and then prepare these practice exams to help you master the textbook material. Unlike study guides, workbooks, and practice tests provided by the texbook publisher and textbook authors, *MznLnx* gives you **all** of the material in each chapter in exam form, not just samples, so you can be sure to nail your exam.

### MECHANICAL

The MznLnx Exam Prep series creates exams that will help you learn the subject matter as well as test you on your understanding. Each question is designed to help you master the concept. Just working through the exams, you gain an understanding of the subject--its a simple mechanical process that produces success.

### INTEGRATED STUDY GUIDE AND REVIEW

MznLnx is not just a set of exams designed to test you, its also a comprehensive review of the subject content. Each exam question is also a review of the concept, making sure that you will get the answer correct without having to go to other sources of material. You learn as you go! Its the easiest way to pass an exam.

### HUMOR

Studying can be tedious and dry. MznLnx's instructional design includes moderate humor within the exam questions on occassion, to break the tedium and revitalize the brain

## Chapter 1. Graphs, Functions, and Models

1. Mathematical _____ is used to represent ideas.
   a. Thing
   b. Notation0
   c. Undefined
   d. Undefined

2. In elementary algebra, an _____ is a set that contains every real number between two indicated numbers and may contain the two numbers themselves.
   a. Interval0
   b. Thing
   c. Undefined
   d. Undefined

3. _____ is the notation in which permitted values for a variable are expressed as ranging over a certain interval; "5 < x < 9" is an example of the application of _____.
   a. Interval notation0
   b. Thing
   c. Undefined
   d. Undefined

4. In mathematics, the _____ (or modulus) of a real number is its numerical value without regard to its sign.
   a. Absolute value0
   b. Thing
   c. Undefined
   d. Undefined

5. _____, from Latin meaning "to make progress", is defined in two different ways. Pure economic _____ is the increase in wealth that an investor has from making an investment, taking into consideration all costs associated with that investment including the opportunity cost of capital.
   a. Thing
   b. Profit0
   c. Undefined
   d. Undefined

6. _____ is a set of numbers, in the broadest sense of the word, together with one or more operations, such as addition or multiplication.
   a. Number system0
   b. Thing
   c. Undefined
   d. Undefined

7. In mathematics, a _____ may be described informally as a number that can be given by an infinite decimal representation.
   a. Real number0
   b. Thing
   c. Undefined
   d. Undefined

8. _____ is a physical property of a system that underlies the common notions of hot and cold; something that is hotter has the greater _____.
   a. Temperature0
   b. Thing
   c. Undefined
   d. Undefined

9. In mathematics, a _____ number is a number which can be expressed as a ratio of two integers. Non-integer _____ numbers (commonly called fractions) are usually written as the vulgar fraction a / b, where b is not zero.
   a. Rational0
   b. Thing
   c. Undefined
   d. Undefined

10. The _____ are the only integral domain whose positive elements are well-ordered, and in which order is preserved by addition. Like the natural numbers, the _____ form a countably infinite set. The set of all _____ is usually denoted in mathematics by a boldface Z .

## Chapter 1. Graphs, Functions, and Models

    a. Integers0                                                 b. Thing
    c. Undefined                                             d. Undefined

11. _____ is the writing of numbers in the base-ten numeral system, which uses various symbols called digits for ten distinct values 0, 1, 2, 3, 4, 5, 6, 7, 8 and 9 to represent numbers
    a. Decimal notation0                                 b. Thing
    c. Undefined                                             d. Undefined

12. In mathematics, an _____ number is any real number that is not a rational number- that is, it is a number which cannot be expressed as a fraction m/n, where m and n are integers.
    a. Irrational0                                           b. Thing
    c. Undefined                                           d. Undefined

13. In mathematics, an _____ is any real number that is not a rational number ¡ª that is, it is a number which cannot be expressed as m/n, where m and n are integers.
    a. Thing                                               b. Irrational number0
    c. Undefined                                         d. Undefined

14. In mathematics, _____ are any real number that is not a rational number ¡ª that is, it is a number which cannot be expressed as m/n, where m and n are integers.
    a. Thing                                               b. Irrational numbers0
    c. Undefined                                         d. Undefined

15. A _____ decimal is a number whose decimal representation eventually becomes periodic (i.e. the same number sequence _____ indefinitely).
    a. Repeating0                                       b. Thing
    c. Undefined                                         d. Undefined

16. A _____ is a one-dimensional picture in which the integers are shown as specially-marked points evenly spaced on a line.
    a. Number line0                                   b. Thing
    c. Undefined                                         d. Undefined

17. In mathematics, an inequality is a statement about the relative size or order of two objects. For example 14 > 10, or 14 is _____ 10.
    a. Greater than0                                  b. Thing
    c. Undefined                                         d. Undefined

18. An _____ or member of a set is an object that when collected together make up the set.
    a. Element0                                        b. Thing
    c. Undefined                                         d. Undefined

19. In mathematics, the _____, or members of a set or more generally a class are all those objects which when collected together make up the set or class.

a. Thing  
b. Elements0  
c. Undefined  
d. Undefined

20. A _____ is a set whose members are members of another set or a set contained within another set.
   a. Thing  
   b. Subset0  
   c. Undefined  
   d. Undefined

21. In geometry, an _____ is a point at which a line segment or ray terminates.
   a. Endpoint0  
   b. Thing  
   c. Undefined  
   d. Undefined

22. _____, either of the curved-bracket punctuation marks that together make a set of _____
   a. Thing  
   b. Parentheses0  
   c. Undefined  
   d. Undefined

23. _____ are the basic objects of study in graph theory. Informally speaking, a graph is a set of objects called points, nodes, or vertices connected by links called lines or edges.
   a. Thing  
   b. Graphs0  
   c. Undefined  
   d. Undefined

24. In mathematics, _____ is an elementary arithmetic operation. When one of the numbers is a whole number, _____ is the repeated sum of the other number.
   a. Multiplication0  
   b. Thing  
   c. Undefined  
   d. Undefined

25. In mathematics, the _____ inverse of a number x, denoted 1/x or $x^{-1}$, is the number which, when multiplied by x, yields 1. The _____ inverse of x is also called the reciprocal of x.
   a. Thing  
   b. Multiplicative0  
   c. Undefined  
   d. Undefined

26. The _____ is a property of multiplication or addition where the product or sum remains the same, regardless of whether or not the order of the addends or factors are changed.
   a. Commutative property0  
   b. Thing  
   c. Undefined  
   d. Undefined

27. An _____ is an equality that remains true regardless of the values of any variables that appear within it, to distinguish it from an equality which is true under more particular conditions.
   a. Thing  
   b. Identity0  
   c. Undefined  
   d. Undefined

28. _____ element of an element x with respect to a binary operation * with identity element e is an element y such that x * y = y * x = e. In particular,
   a. Thing  
   b. Inverse0  
   c. Undefined  
   d. Undefined

29. In mathematics, the _____ inverse, or opposite, of a number n is the number that, when added to n, yields zero. The _____ inverse of n is denoted −n.
    a. Thing
    b. Additive0
    c. Undefined
    d. Undefined

30. In mathematics the _____ of a set which is equipped with the operation of addition is an element which, when added to any other element x in the set, yields x.
    a. Concept
    b. Additive identity0
    c. Undefined
    d. Undefined

31. In mathematics, the _____ of a number n is the number that, when added to n, yields zero. The _____ of n is denoted −n. For example, 7 is −7, because 7 + (−7) = 0, and the _____ of −0.3 is 0.3, because −0.3 + 0.3 = 0.
    a. Additive inverse0
    b. Thing
    c. Undefined
    d. Undefined

32. The _____ states that - a number and its additive inverse have a sum of zero (0).
    a. Concept
    b. Additive inverse property0
    c. Undefined
    d. Undefined

33. In mathematics, and in particular in abstract algebra, the _____ is a property of binary operations that generalises the distributive law from elementary algebra.
    a. Thing
    b. Distributive property0
    c. Undefined
    d. Undefined

34. In mathematics, _____ is a property that a binary operation can have. Within an expression containing two or more of the same associative operators in a row, the order of operations does not matter as long as the sequence of the operands is not changed.
    a. Thing
    b. Associativity0
    c. Undefined
    d. Undefined

35. _____ is a branch of mathematics concerning the study of structure, relation and quantity.
    a. Algebra0
    b. Concept
    c. Undefined
    d. Undefined

36. The _____ integers are all the integers from zero on upwards.
    a. Nonnegative0
    b. Thing
    c. Undefined
    d. Undefined

37. In mathematics, the additive inverse, or _____ of a number n is the number that, when added to n, yields zero. The additive inverse of n is denoted −n. For example, 7 is −7, because 7 + (−7) = 0, and the additive inverse of −0.3 is 0.3, because −0.3 + 0.3 = 0.
    a. Thing
    b. Opposite0
    c. Undefined
    d. Undefined

38. A _____ is one of the basic shapes of geometry: a polygon with three vertices and three sides which are straight line segments.

## Chapter 1. Graphs, Functions, and Models

  a. Triangle0              b. Thing
  c. Undefined             d. Undefined

39.  The _____ of measurement are a globally standardized and modernized form of the metric system.
  a. Units0               b. Thing
  c. Undefined             d. Undefined

40.  A _____ is a function that assigns a number to subsets of a given set.
  a. Thing               b. Measure0
  c. Undefined             d. Undefined

41.  _____ has one 90° internal angle a right angle.
  a. Right triangle0           b. Thing
  c. Undefined             d. Undefined

42.  In arithmetic and algebra, when a number or expression is both preceded and followed by a binary operation, an _____ is required for which operation should be applied first.
  a. Thing               b. Order of operations0
  c. Undefined             d. Undefined

43.  _____ is a mathematical operation, written $a^n$, involving two numbers, the base a and the exponent n.
  a. Thing               b. Exponentiating0
  c. Undefined             d. Undefined

44.  _____ is a mathematical operation, written $a^n$, involving two numbers, the base a and the exponent n.
  a. Thing               b. Exponentiation0
  c. Undefined             d. Undefined

45.  An _____ is a combination of numbers, operators, grouping symbols and/or free variables and bound variables arranged in a meaningful way which can be evaluated..
  a. Thing               b. Expression0
  c. Undefined             d. Undefined

46.  _____ is a notation for writing numbers that is often used by scientists and mathematicians to make it easier to write large and small numbers.
  a. Scientific notation0          b. Thing
  c. Undefined             d. Undefined

47.  In mathematics, a _____ is the result of multiplying, or an expression that identifies factors to be multiplied.
  a. Thing               b. Product0
  c. Undefined             d. Undefined

48.  In geometry, the _____ of an object is a point in some sense in the middle of the object.
  a. Center0              b. Thing
  c. Undefined             d. Undefined

## Chapter 1. Graphs, Functions, and Models

49. _____ is a mathematical science pertaining to the collection, analysis, interpretation or explanation, and presentation of data. It is applicable to a wide variety of academic disciplines, from the physical and social sciences to the humanities.
   a. Statistics0
   b. Thing
   c. Undefined
   d. Undefined

50. The decimal separator is a symbol used to mark the boundary between the integral and the fractional parts of a decimal numeral. Terms implying the symbol used are _____ and decimal comma.
   a. Concept
   b. Decimal point0
   c. Undefined
   d. Undefined

51. _____ is the property of a physical object that quantifies the amount of matter and energy it is equivalent to.
   a. Thing
   b. Mass0
   c. Undefined
   d. Undefined

52. _____ is electromagnetic radiation with a wavelength that is visible to the eye (visible _____) or, in a technical or scientific context, electromagnetic radiation of any wavelength.
   a. Thing
   b. Light0
   c. Undefined
   d. Undefined

53. _____ is the transport of people on a trip/journey or the process or time involved in a person or object moving from one location to another.
   a. Travel0
   b. Thing
   c. Undefined
   d. Undefined

54. A _____ is a unit of length, usually used to measure distance, in a number of different systems, including Imperial units, United States customary units and Norwegian/Swedish mil. Its size can vary from system to system, but in each is between 1 and 10 kilometers. In contemporary English contexts _____ refers to either:
   a. Mile0
   b. Thing
   c. Undefined
   d. Undefined

55. In abstract algebra, _____ consists of sets with binary operations that satisfy certain axioms.
   a. Thing
   b. Grouping0
   c. Undefined
   d. Undefined

56. _____ are objects, characters, or other concrete representations of ideas, concepts, or other abstractions.
   a. Thing
   b. Symbols0
   c. Undefined
   d. Undefined

57. A _____ is a deliberate process for transforming one or more inputs into one or more results.
   a. Thing
   b. Calculation0
   c. Undefined
   d. Undefined

58. In mathematics, _____ growth occurs when the growth rate of a function is always proportional to the function's current size.

## Chapter 1. Graphs, Functions, and Models

a. Exponential0
b. Thing
c. Undefined
d. Undefined

59. The _____ (symbol _____) and the millibar (symbol mbar, also mb) are units of pressure.
a. Thing
b. Bar0
c. Undefined
d. Undefined

60. A _____ is a special kind of ratio, indicating a relationship between two measurements with different units, such as miles to gallons or cents to pounds.
a. Thing
b. Rate0
c. Undefined
d. Undefined

61. _____ is a kind of property which exists as magnitude or multitude. It is among the basic classes of things along with quality, substance, change, and relation.
a. Amount0
b. Thing
c. Undefined
d. Undefined

62. _____ is the fee paid on borrowed money.
a. Thing
b. Interest0
c. Undefined
d. Undefined

63. An _____ is the fee paid on borrow money.
a. Interest rate0
b. Concept
c. Undefined
d. Undefined

64. A _____ is a numeral used to indicate a count. The most common use of the word today is to name the part of a fraction that tells the number or count of equal parts.
a. Numerator0
b. Thing
c. Undefined
d. Undefined

65. A _____ is the part of a fraction that tells how many equal parts make up a whole, and which is used in the name of the fraction: "halves", "thirds", "fourths" or "quarters", "fifths" and so on.
a. Denominator0
b. Concept
c. Undefined
d. Undefined

66. Compass and straightedge or ruler-and-compass _____ is the _____ of lengths or angles using only an idealized ruler and compass.
a. Thing
b. Construction0
c. Undefined
d. Undefined

67. In plane geometry, a _____ is a polygon with four equal sides, four right angles, and parallel opposite sides. In algebra, the _____ of a number is that number multiplied by itself.
a. Square0
b. Thing
c. Undefined
d. Undefined

## Chapter 1. Graphs, Functions, and Models

68. In sociology and biology a _____ is the collection of people or organisms of a particular species living in a given geographic area or space, usually measured by a census.
    a. Population0
    b. Thing
    c. Undefined
    d. Undefined

69. _____ interest refers to the fact that whenever interest is calculated, it is based not only on the original principal, but also on any unpaid interest that has been added to the principal.
    a. Thing
    b. Compound0
    c. Undefined
    d. Undefined

70. _____ refers to the fact that whenever interest is calculated, it is based not only on the original principal, but also on any unpaid interest that has been added to the principal. The more frequently interest is compounded, the faster the balance grows.
    a. Compound interest0
    b. Concept
    c. Undefined
    d. Undefined

71. _____ has many meanings, most of which simply .
    a. Thing
    b. Power0
    c. Undefined
    d. Undefined

72. In mathematics, a _____ is a constant multiplicative factor of a certain object. The object can be such things as a variable, a vector, a function, etc. For example, the _____ of $9x^2$ is 9.
    a. Coefficient0
    b. Thing
    c. Undefined
    d. Undefined

73. In mathematics, a _____ is an expression that is constructed from one or more variables and constants, using only the operations of addition, subtraction, multiplication, and constant positive whole number exponents. is a _____. Note in particular that division by an expression containing a variable is not in general allowed in polynomials. [1]
    a. Thing
    b. Polynomial0
    c. Undefined
    d. Undefined

74. A _____ is a symbolic representation denoting a quantity or expression. It often represents an "unknown" quantity that has the potential to change.
    a. Thing
    b. Variable0
    c. Undefined
    d. Undefined

75. In mathematics, there are several meanings of _____ depending on the subject.
    a. Degree0
    b. Thing
    c. Undefined
    d. Undefined

76. In mathematics and the mathematical sciences, a _____ is a fixed, but possibly unspecified, value. This is in contrast to a variable, which is not fixed.
    a. Constant0
    b. Thing
    c. Undefined
    d. Undefined

77. _____ is a fixed, but possibly unspecified, value. This is in contrast to a variable, which is not fixed.

a. Constant term0  
b. Thing  
c. Undefined  
d. Undefined

78. A _____ is the result of the addition of a set of numbers. The numbers may be natural numbers, complex numbers, matrices, or still more complicated objects. An infinite _____ is a subtle procedure known as a series.
   a. Thing  
   b. Sum0  
   c. Undefined  
   d. Undefined

79. The _____ is the sum of the exponents of the variables in the term.
   a. Degree of a term0  
   b. Thing  
   c. Undefined  
   d. Undefined

80. The _____ is the maximum of the degrees of all terms in the polynomial.
   a. Degree of a polynomial0  
   b. Thing  
   c. Undefined  
   d. Undefined

81. In elementary algebra, a _____ is a polynomial with two terms: the sum of two monomials. It is the simplest kind of polynomial except for a monomial.
   a. Thing  
   b. Binomial0  
   c. Undefined  
   d. Undefined

82. A _____ is a polynomial consisting of three terms; in other words, it is the sum of three monomials.
   a. Trinomial0  
   b. Thing  
   c. Undefined  
   d. Undefined

83. _____ is the largest positive integer that divides both numbers without remainder.
   a. Common Factor0  
   b. Thing  
   c. Undefined  
   d. Undefined

84. _____ also sometimes known as the double distributive property or more colloquially as foiling, is commonly taught to US high school students learning algebra as a mnemonic for remembering how to multiply two binomials polynomials with two terms.
   a. FOIL method0  
   b. Thing  
   c. Undefined  
   d. Undefined

85. The _____ is commonly taught to US high school students learning algebra as a mnemonic for remembering how to multiply two binomials.
   a. Thing  
   b. FOIL rule0  
   c. Undefined  
   d. Undefined

86. Equivalence is the condition of being _____ or essentially equal.
   a. Thing  
   b. Equivalent0  
   c. Undefined  
   d. Undefined

## Chapter 1. Graphs, Functions, and Models

87. In mathematics, factorization (British English: factorisation) or factoring is the decomposition of an object (for example, a number, a polynomial, or a matrix) into a product of other objects, or _____, which when multiplied together give the original.
   a. Factors0
   b. Thing
   c. Undefined
   d. Undefined

88. A _____ is a negotiable instrument instructing a financial institution to pay a specific amount of a specific currency from a specific demand account held in the maker/depositor's name with that institution. Both the maker and payee may be natural persons or legal entities.
   a. Thing
   b. Check0
   c. Undefined
   d. Undefined

89. In mathematics, _____ is the decomposition of an object into a product of other objects, or factors, which when multiplied together give the original.
   a. Thing
   b. Factoring0
   c. Undefined
   d. Undefined

90. In mathematics, the conjugate _____ or adjoint matrix of an m-by-n matrix A with complex entries is the n-by-m matrix A* obtained from A by taking the transpose and then taking the complex conjugate of each entry.
   a. Pairs0
   b. Thing
   c. Undefined
   d. Undefined

91. In combinatorial mathematics, a _____ is an un-ordered collection of unique elements.
   a. Combination0
   b. Concept
   c. Undefined
   d. Undefined

92. A _____ is a three-dimensional solid object bounded by six square faces, facets, or sides, with three meeting at each vertex.
   a. Thing
   b. Cube0
   c. Undefined
   d. Undefined

93. _____ are of a number n in its third power-the result of multiplying it by itself three times.
   a. Thing
   b. Cubes0
   c. Undefined
   d. Undefined

94. In mathematics, a _____ can mean either an element of the set {1, 2, 3, ...} (i.e the positive integers or the counting numbers) or an element of the set {0, 1, 2, 3, ...} (i.e. the non-negative integers).
   a. Thing
   b. Natural number0
   c. Undefined
   d. Undefined

95. In mathematics, a _____ of a k-place relation $L \subseteq X_1 \times ... \times X_k$ is one of the sets $X_j$, $1 \le j \le k$. In the special case where k = 2 and $L \subseteq X_1 \times X_2$ is a function $L : X_1 \to X_2$, it is conventional to refer to $X_1$ as the _____ of the function and to refer to $X_2$ as the codomain of the function.
   a. Thing
   b. Domain0
   c. Undefined
   d. Undefined

96. In mathematics, a _____ is the end result of a division problem. It can also be expressed as the number of times the divisor divides into the dividend.
   a. Thing
   b. Quotient0
   c. Undefined
   d. Undefined

97. In mathematics, the multiplicative inverse of a number x, denoted 1/x or $x^{-1}$, is the number which, when multiplied by x, yields 1. The multiplicative inverse of x is also called the _____ of x.
   a. Thing
   b. Reciprocal0
   c. Undefined
   d. Undefined

98. In mathematics, a _____ of an integer n, also called a factor of n, is an integer which evenly divides n without leaving a remainder.
   a. Divisor0
   b. Thing
   c. Undefined
   d. Undefined

99. _____ is the symbold used to indicate the nth root of a number
   a. Thing
   b. Radical0
   c. Undefined
   d. Undefined

100. In mathematics, a _____ of a number x is a number r such that $r^2 = x$, or in words, a number r whose square (the result of multiplying the number by itself) is x.
   a. Square root0
   b. Thing
   c. Undefined
   d. Undefined

101. In mathematics, a _____ of a complex-valued function f is a member x of the domain of f such that f(x) vanishes at x, that is, x : f (x) = 0.
   a. Root0
   b. Thing
   c. Undefined
   d. Undefined

102. An _____ of a number a is a number b such that $b^n = a$.
   a. Thing
   b. Nth root0
   c. Undefined
   d. Undefined

103. A _____ of a number is a number a such that $a^3 = x$.
   a. Thing
   b. Cube root0
   c. Undefined
   d. Undefined

104. The _____ is the number or expression underneath the radical sign.
   a. Radicand0
   b. Thing
   c. Undefined
   d. Undefined

105. The word _____ is used in a variety of ways in mathematics.
   a. Thing
   b. Index0
   c. Undefined
   d. Undefined

106. In geographic information systems, a _____ comprises an entity with a geographic location, typically determined by points, arcs, or polygons. Carriageways and cadastres exemplify _____ data.
   a. Feature0
   b. Thing
   c. Undefined
   d. Undefined

107. In mathematics, _____ are used to indicate the square root of a number.
   a. Radicals0
   b. Thing
   c. Undefined
   d. Undefined

108. _____ is a relation in Euclidean geometry among the three sides of a right triangle.
   a. Thing
   b. Pythagorean Theorem0
   c. Undefined
   d. Undefined

109. In mathematics, a _____ is a statement that can be proved on the basis of explicitly stated or previously agreed assumptions.
   a. Theorem0
   b. Thing
   c. Undefined
   d. Undefined

110. The _____ of a right triangle is the triangle's longest side; the side opposite the right angle.
   a. Hypotenuse0
   b. Thing
   c. Undefined
   d. Undefined

111. In geometry and trigonometry, a _____ is defined as an angle between two straight intersecting lines of ninety degrees, or one-quarter of a circle.
   a. Right angle0
   b. Thing
   c. Undefined
   d. Undefined

112. In a right triangle, the _____ of the triangle are the two sides that are perpendicular to each other, as opposed to the hypotenuse.
   a. Legs0
   b. Thing
   c. Undefined
   d. Undefined

113. _____, or Rationalisation in mathematics is the process of removing a square root or imaginary number from the denominator of a fraction.
   a. Rationalizing0
   b. Thing
   c. Undefined
   d. Undefined

114. In algebra, a _____ is a binomial formed by taking the opposite of the second term of a binomial.
   a. Conjugate0
   b. Thing
   c. Undefined
   d. Undefined

115. In geometry, an _____ of a triangle is a straight line through a vertex and perpendicular to (i.e. forming a right angle with) the opposite side or an extension of the opposite side.
   a. Altitude0
   b. Concept
   c. Undefined
   d. Undefined

## Chapter 1. Graphs, Functions, and Models

116. A _____ can refer to a line joining two nonadjacent vertices of a polygon or polyhedron, or in some contexts any upward or downward sloping line. .
   a. Thing
   b. Diagonal0
   c. Undefined
   d. Undefined

117. _____ is the middle point of a line segment.
   a. Midpoint0
   b. Thing
   c. Undefined
   d. Undefined

118. An _____ triange is a triangle with at least two sides of equal length.
   a. Isosceles0
   b. Thing
   c. Undefined
   d. Undefined

119. The _____ governs the differentiation of products of differentiable functions.
   a. Thing
   b. Product rule0
   c. Undefined
   d. Undefined

120. The _____ is a method of finding the derivative of a function that is the quotient of two other functions for which derivatives exist.
   a. Thing
   b. Quotient rule0
   c. Undefined
   d. Undefined

121. A _____ is a method of using property as security for the payment of a debt.
   a. Thing
   b. Mortgage0
   c. Undefined
   d. Undefined

122. A _____ is a type of debt. All material things can be lent but this article focuses exclusively on monetary loans. Like all debt instruments, a _____ entails the redistribution of financial assets over time, between the lender and the borrower.
   a. Thing
   b. Loan0
   c. Undefined
   d. Undefined

123. In business, particularly accounting, a _____ is the time intervals that the accounts, statement, payments, or other calculations cover.
   a. Period0
   b. Thing
   c. Undefined
   d. Undefined

## Chapter 2. Functions, Equations, and Inequalities

1. _____ are the basic objects of study in graph theory. Informally speaking, a graph is a set of objects called points, nodes, or vertices connected by links called lines or edges.
   a. Graphs0
   b. Thing
   c. Undefined
   d. Undefined

2. A _____ is a special kind of ratio, indicating a relationship between two measurements with different units, such as miles to gallons or cents to pounds.
   a. Rate0
   b. Thing
   c. Undefined
   d. Undefined

3. In mathematics, an _____, mean, or central tendency of a data set refers to a measure of the "middle" or "expected" value of the data set.
   a. Concept
   b. Average0
   c. Undefined
   d. Undefined

4. The mathematical concept of a _____ expresses the intuitive idea of deterministic dependence between two quantities, one of which is viewed as primary and the other as secondary. A _____ then is a way to associate a unique output for each input of a specified type, for example, a real number or an element of a given set.
   a. Function0
   b. Thing
   c. Undefined
   d. Undefined

5. _____ is a synonym for information.
   a. Data0
   b. Thing
   c. Undefined
   d. Undefined

6. The _____, the average in everyday English, which is also called the arithmetic _____ (and is distinguished from the geometric _____ or harmonic _____). The average is also called the sample _____. The expected value of a random variable, which is also called the population _____.
   a. Thing
   b. Mean0
   c. Undefined
   d. Undefined

7. _____ is the level of functional and/or metabolic efficiency of an organism at both the micro level.
   a. Thing
   b. Health0
   c. Undefined
   d. Undefined

8. _____, in law and economics, is a form of risk management primarily used to hedge against the risk of a contingent loss.
   a. Insurance0
   b. Thing
   c. Undefined
   d. Undefined

9. _____ is a type of insurance whereby the insurer pays the medical costs of the insured if the insured becomes sick due to covered causes, or due to accidents.
   a. Medical insurance0
   b. Thing
   c. Undefined
   d. Undefined

10. A _____ is a symbolic representation denoting a quantity or expression. It often represents an "unknown" quantity that has the potential to change.

## Chapter 2. Functions, Equations, and Inequalities

a. Variable0
b. Thing
c. Undefined
d. Undefined

11. A _____ is a one-dimensional picture in which the integers are shown as specially-marked points evenly spaced on a line.
a. Thing
b. Number line0
c. Undefined
d. Undefined

12. An _____ is when two lines intersect somewhere on a plane creating a right angle at intersection
a. Axes0
b. Thing
c. Undefined
d. Undefined

13. In mathematics, the _____ of a coordinate system is the point where the axes of the system intersect.
a. Thing
b. Origin0
c. Undefined
d. Undefined

14. In mathematics, a _____ is a two-dimensional manifold or surface that is perfectly flat.
a. Thing
b. Plane0
c. Undefined
d. Undefined

15. An _____ is a straight line around which a geometric figure can be rotated.
a. Thing
b. Axis0
c. Undefined
d. Undefined

16. In astronomy, geography, geometry and related sciences and contexts, a plane is said to be _____ at a given point if it is locally perpendicular to the gradient of the gravity field, i.e., with the direction of the gravitational force at that point.
a. Horizontal0
b. Thing
c. Undefined
d. Undefined

17. A _____ consists of one quarter of the coordinate plane.
a. Thing
b. Quadrant0
c. Undefined
d. Undefined

18. A _____ is a symbol or group of symbols, or a word in a natural language that represents a number.
a. Thing
b. Numeral0
c. Undefined
d. Undefined

19. An _____ is a collection of two not necessarily distinct objects, one of which is distinguished as the first coordinate and the other as the second coordinate.
a. Thing
b. Ordered pair0
c. Undefined
d. Undefined

20. A _____ is a set of numbers that designate location in a given reference system, such as x,y in a planar _____ system or an x,y,z in a three-dimensional _____ system.

# Chapter 2. Functions, Equations, and Inequalities

a. Thing  
b. Coordinate0  
c. Undefined  
d. Undefined

21. The _____ of measurement are a globally standardized and modernized form of the metric system.
    a. Units0  
    b. Thing  
    c. Undefined  
    d. Undefined

22. Mathematical _____ is used to represent ideas.
    a. Notation0  
    b. Thing  
    c. Undefined  
    d. Undefined

23. In elementary algebra, an _____ is a set that contains every real number between two indicated numbers and may contain the two numbers themselves.
    a. Thing  
    b. Interval0  
    c. Undefined  
    d. Undefined

24. _____ is the state of being greater than any finite real or natural number, however large.
    a. Thing  
    b. Infinite0  
    c. Undefined  
    d. Undefined

25. Any point where a graph makes contact with an coordinate axis is called an _____ of the graph
    a. Thing  
    b. Intercept0  
    c. Undefined  
    d. Undefined

26. A _____ is a negotiable instrument instructing a financial institution to pay a specific amount of a specific currency from a specific demand account held in the maker/depositor's name with that institution. Both the maker and payee may be natural persons or legal entities.
    a. Thing  
    b. Check0  
    c. Undefined  
    d. Undefined

27. In mathematics, the conjugate _____ or adjoint matrix of an m-by-n matrix A with complex entries is the n-by-m matrix A* obtained from A by taking the transpose and then taking the complex conjugate of each entry.
    a. Pairs0  
    b. Thing  
    c. Undefined  
    d. Undefined

28. In Euclidean geometry, a uniform _____ is a linear transformation that enlargers or diminishes objects, and whose _____ factor is the same in all directions. This is also called homothethy.
    a. Scale0  
    b. Thing  
    c. Undefined  
    d. Undefined

29. A _____ of a number is the product of that number with any integer.
    a. Thing  
    b. Multiple0  
    c. Undefined  
    d. Undefined

30. In mathematics, an _____ is any of the arguments, i.e. "inputs", to a function. Thus if we have a function f(x), then x is a _____.

## Chapter 2. Functions, Equations, and Inequalities 17

a. Independent variable0  
c. Undefined  
b. Thing  
d. Undefined

31. In a function the _____ is the variable which is the value, i.e. the "output", of the function.
    a. Thing
    b. Dependent variable0
    c. Undefined
    d. Undefined

32. In geographic information systems, a _____ comprises an entity with a geographic location, typically determined by points, arcs, or polygons. Carriageways and cadastres exemplify _____ data.
    a. Feature0
    b. Thing
    c. Undefined
    d. Undefined

33. In geometry, an _____ is a point at which a line segment or ray terminates.
    a. Endpoint0
    b. Thing
    c. Undefined
    d. Undefined

34. _____ is a relation in Euclidean geometry among the three sides of a right triangle.
    a. Thing
    b. Pythagorean Theorem0
    c. Undefined
    d. Undefined

35. The _____ of a right triangle is the triangle's longest side; the side opposite the right angle.
    a. Thing
    b. Hypotenuse0
    c. Undefined
    d. Undefined

36. In mathematics, a _____ is a statement that can be proved on the basis of explicitly stated or previously agreed assumptions.
    a. Thing
    b. Theorem0
    c. Undefined
    d. Undefined

37. In geometry, the _____ of an object is a point in some sense in the middle of the object.
    a. Center0
    b. Thing
    c. Undefined
    d. Undefined

38. In Euclidean geometry, a _____ is the set of all points in a plane at a fixed distance, called the radius, from a given point, the center.
    a. Circle0
    b. Thing
    c. Undefined
    d. Undefined

39. In geometry, a line _____ is a part of a line that is bounded by two end points, and contains every point on the line between its end points.
    a. Concept
    b. Segment0
    c. Undefined
    d. Undefined

40. In classical geometry, a _____ of a circle or sphere is any line segment from its center to its boundary. By extension, the _____ of a circle or sphere is the length of any such segment. The _____ is half the diameter. In science and engineering the term _____ of curvature is commonly used as a synonym for _____.

## Chapter 2. Functions, Equations, and Inequalities

    a. Radius0  
    b. Thing  
    c. Undefined  
    d. Undefined

41. _____ the expected value of a random variable displays the average or central value of the variable. It is a summary value of the distribution of the variable.
    a. Determining0
    b. Thing
    c. Undefined
    d. Undefined

42. _____ is the middle point of a line segment.
    a. Midpoint0
    b. Thing
    c. Undefined
    d. Undefined

43. In geometry, a _____ (Greek words diairo = divide and metro = measure) of a circle is any straight line segment that passes through the centre and whose endpoints are on the circular boundary, or, in more modern usage, the length of such a line segment. When using the word in the more modern sense, one speaks of the _____ rather than a _____, because all diameters of a circle have the same length. This length is twice the radius. The _____ of a circle is also the longest chord that the circle has.
    a. Diameter0
    b. Thing
    c. Undefined
    d. Undefined

44. _____ is a notation for writing numbers that is often used by scientists and mathematicians to make it easier to write large and small numbers.
    a. Scientific notation0
    b. Thing
    c. Undefined
    d. Undefined

45. In plane geometry, a _____ is a polygon with four equal sides, four right angles, and parallel opposite sides. In algebra, the _____ of a number is that number multiplied by itself.
    a. Thing
    b. Square0
    c. Undefined
    d. Undefined

46. One of the three formats applicable to a quadratic function is the _____ which is defined as $f = ax^2 + bx + c$.
    a. Thing
    b. General form0
    c. Undefined
    d. Undefined

47. _____, either of the curved-bracket punctuation marks that together make a set of _____
    a. Thing
    b. Parentheses0
    c. Undefined
    d. Undefined

48. In mathematics, _____ expressions is used to reduce the expression into the lowest possible term.
    a. Thing
    b. Simplifying0
    c. Undefined
    d. Undefined

49. A _____ is a quantity that denotes the proportional amount or magnitude of one quantity relative to another.
    a. Thing
    b. Ratio0
    c. Undefined
    d. Undefined

## Chapter 2. Functions, Equations, and Inequalities

50. _____ is a kind of property which exists as magnitude or multitude. It is among the basic classes of things along with quality, substance, change, and relation.
   a. Amount0
   b. Thing
   c. Undefined
   d. Undefined

51. _____ Logic is a concept in traditional logic referring to a "type of immediate inference in which from a given proposition another proposition is inferred which has as its subject the predicate of the original proposition and as its predicate the subject of the original proposition (the quality of the proposition being retained)."
   a. Converse0
   b. Concept
   c. Undefined
   d. Undefined

52. In common philosophical language, a proposition or _____, is the content of an assertion, that is, it is true-or-false and defined by the meaning of a particular piece of language.
   a. Concept
   b. Statement0
   c. Undefined
   d. Undefined

53. A _____ is one of the basic shapes of geometry: a polygon with three vertices and three sides which are straight line segments.
   a. Thing
   b. Triangle0
   c. Undefined
   d. Undefined

54. A _____ is the result of the addition of a set of numbers. The numbers may be natural numbers, complex numbers, matrices, or still more complicated objects. An infinite _____ is a subtle procedure known as a series.
   a. Sum0
   b. Thing
   c. Undefined
   d. Undefined

55. _____ has one 90° internal angle a right angle.
   a. Thing
   b. Right triangle0
   c. Undefined
   d. Undefined

56. In geometry, a _____ is a special kind of point, usually a corner of a polygon, polyhedron, or higher dimensional polytope. In the geometry of curves a _____ is a point of where the first derivative of curvature is zero. In graph theory, a _____ is the fundamental unit out of which graphs are formed
   a. Thing
   b. Vertex0
   c. Undefined
   d. Undefined

57. A _____ is a polygon with four sides and four vertices.
   a. Quadrilateral0
   b. Thing
   c. Undefined
   d. Undefined

58. A _____ can refer to a line joining two nonadjacent vertices of a polygon or polyhedron, or in some contexts any upward or downward sloping line. .
   a. Thing
   b. Diagonal0
   c. Undefined
   d. Undefined

## Chapter 2. Functions, Equations, and Inequalities

59. In trigonometry, the _____ is a function defined as $\tan x = \sin x / \cos x$. The function is so-named because it can be defined as the length of a certain segment of a _____ (in the geometric sense) to the unit circle. In plane geometry, a line is _____ to a curve, at some point, if both line and curve pass through the point with the same direction.
   a. Thing
   b. Tangent0
   c. Undefined
   d. Undefined

60. The _____ is the distance around a closed curve. _____ is a kind of perimeter.
   a. Circumference0
   b. Thing
   c. Undefined
   d. Undefined

61. Three or more points that lie on the same line are called _____.
   a. Thing
   b. Collinear0
   c. Undefined
   d. Undefined

62. _____ is the estimation of a physical quantity such as distance, energy, temperature, or time.
   a. Measurement0
   b. Thing
   c. Undefined
   d. Undefined

63. In mathematics and its applications, a _____ is a system for assigning an n-tuple of numbers or scalars to each point in an n-dimensional space.
   a. Concept
   b. Coordinate system0
   c. Undefined
   d. Undefined

64. A _____ is a unit of length, usually used to measure distance, in a number of different systems, including Imperial units, United States customary units and Norwegian/Swedish mil. Its size can vary from system to system, but in each is between 1 and 10 kilometers. In contemporary English contexts _____ refers to either:
   a. Thing
   b. Mile0
   c. Undefined
   d. Undefined

65. A _____ is a landform that extends above the surrounding terrain in a limited area. A _____ is generally steeper than a hill, but there is no universally accepted standard definition for the height of a _____ or a hill although a _____ usually has an identifiable summit.
   a. Thing
   b. Mountain0
   c. Undefined
   d. Undefined

66. In mathematics, the _____ of a function is the set of all "output" values produced by that function. Given a function $f : A \to B$, the _____ of $f$, is defined to be the set $\{x \in B : x = f(a) \text{ for some } a \in A\}$.
   a. Thing
   b. Range0
   c. Undefined
   d. Undefined

67. In mathematics, a _____ of a k-place relation $L \subseteq X_1 \times \ldots \times X_k$ is one of the sets $X_j$, $1 \le j \le k$. In the special case where $k = 2$ and $L \subseteq X_1 \times X_2$ is a function $L : X_1 \to X_2$, it is conventional to refer to $X_1$ as the _____ of the function and to refer to $X_2$ as the codomain of the function.
   a. Thing
   b. Domain0
   c. Undefined
   d. Undefined

## Chapter 2. Functions, Equations, and Inequalities

68. In physics, _____ is an influence that may cause an object to accelerate. It may be experienced as a lift, a push, or a pull. The actual acceleration of the body is determined by the vector sum of all forces acting on it, known as net _____ or resultant _____.
   a. Thing
   b. Force0
   c. Undefined
   d. Undefined

69. A _____ is a three-dimensional solid object bounded by six square faces, facets, or sides, with three meeting at each vertex.
   a. Thing
   b. Cube0
   c. Undefined
   d. Undefined

70. A _____ of a number is a number a such that $a^3 = x$.
   a. Thing
   b. Cube root0
   c. Undefined
   d. Undefined

71. In mathematics, a _____ may be described informally as a number that can be given by an infinite decimal representation.
   a. Thing
   b. Real number0
   c. Undefined
   d. Undefined

72. A _____ is a set whose members are members of another set or a set contained within another set.
   a. Thing
   b. Subset0
   c. Undefined
   d. Undefined

73. The _____ are the only integral domain whose positive elements are well-ordered, and in which order is preserved by addition. Like the natural numbers, the _____ form a countably infinite set. The set of all _____ is usually denoted in mathematics by a boldface Z .
   a. Thing
   b. Integers0
   c. Undefined
   d. Undefined

74. In mathematics, a _____ of a complex-valued function f is a member x of the domain of f such that f(x) vanishes at x, that is, $x : f(x) = 0$.
   a. Thing
   b. Root0
   c. Undefined
   d. Undefined

75. In mathematics, the concept of a _____ tries to capture the intuitive idea of a geometrical one-dimensional and continuous object. A simple example is the circle.
   a. Thing
   b. Curve0
   c. Undefined
   d. Undefined

76. In mathematics, the _____ f is the collection of all ordered pairs . In particular, graph means the graphical representation of this collection, in the form of a curve or surface, together with axes, etc. Graphing on a Cartesian plane is sometimes referred to as curve sketching.
   a. Thing
   b. Graph of a function0
   c. Undefined
   d. Undefined

## Chapter 2. Functions, Equations, and Inequalities

77. Acid _____ ratio measures the ability of a company to use its near cash or quick assets to immediately extinguish its current liabilities.
   a. Thing
   b. Test0
   c. Undefined
   d. Undefined

78. In mathematics, _____ geometry was the traditional name for the geometry of three-dimensional Euclidean space — for practical purposes the kind of space we live in.
   a. Thing
   b. Solid0
   c. Undefined
   d. Undefined

79. An _____ is a combination of numbers, operators, grouping symbols and/or free variables and bound variables arranged in a meaningful way which can be evaluated..
   a. Thing
   b. Expression0
   c. Undefined
   d. Undefined

80. A _____ is the part of a fraction that tells how many equal parts make up a whole, and which is used in the name of the fraction: "halves", "thirds", "fourths" or "quarters", "fifths" and so on.
   a. Concept
   b. Denominator0
   c. Undefined
   d. Undefined

81. _____ is the notation in which permitted values for a variable are expressed as ranging over a certain interval; "5 < x < 9" is an example of the application of _____.
   a. Interval notation0
   b. Thing
   c. Undefined
   d. Undefined

82. A _____ is a numeral used to indicate a count. The most common use of the word today is to name the part of a fraction that tells the number or count of equal parts.
   a. Thing
   b. Numerator0
   c. Undefined
   d. Undefined

83. _____ is a temperature scale named after the German physicist Daniel Gabriel _____ , who proposed it in 1724.
   a. Thing
   b. Fahrenheit0
   c. Undefined
   d. Undefined

84. In mathematics, there are several meanings of _____ depending on the subject.
   a. Thing
   b. Degree0
   c. Undefined
   d. Undefined

85. _____ is a physical property of a system that underlies the common notions of hot and cold; something that is hotter has the greater _____.
   a. Temperature0
   b. Thing
   c. Undefined
   d. Undefined

86. _____ is a unit of speed, expressing the number of international miles covered per hour.

a. Thing  
b. Miles per hour0  
c. Undefined  
d. Undefined

87. An _____ is the result from the sudden release of stored energy in the Earth's crust that creates seismic waves.
a. Earthquake0  
b. Thing  
c. Undefined  
d. Undefined

88. In mathematics, an _____ is a statement about the relative size or order of two objects.
a. Inequality0  
b. Thing  
c. Undefined  
d. Undefined

89. The word _____ comes from the Latin word linearis, which means created by lines.
a. Linear0  
b. Thing  
c. Undefined  
d. Undefined

90. A _____ is an abstract model that uses mathematical language to describe the behavior of a system. Eykhoff defined a _____ as 'a representation of the essential aspects of an existing system which presents knowledge of that system in usable form'.
a. Thing  
b. Mathematical model0  
c. Undefined  
d. Undefined

91. A _____ is a first degree polynomial mathematical function of the form: f(x) = mx + b where m and b are real constants and x is a real variable.
a. Linear function0  
b. Thing  
c. Undefined  
d. Undefined

92. _____ systems represent systems whose behavior is not expressible as a sum of the behaviors of its descriptors.
a. Nonlinear0  
b. Thing  
c. Undefined  
d. Undefined

93. _____ is often used to describe the measurement of the steepness, incline, gradient, or grade of a straight line. The _____ is defined as the ratio of the "rise" divided by the "run" between two points on a line, or in other words, the ratio of the altitude change to the horizontal distance between any two points on the line.
a. Slope0  
b. Thing  
c. Undefined  
d. Undefined

94. In mathematics and the mathematical sciences, a _____ is a fixed, but possibly unspecified, value. This is in contrast to a variable, which is not fixed.
a. Thing  
b. Constant0  
c. Undefined  
d. Undefined

95. _____ is a function whose values do not vary and thus are constant.
a. Constant function0  
b. Thing  
c. Undefined  
d. Undefined

# Chapter 2. Functions, Equations, and Inequalities

96. An _____ is an equality that remains true regardless of the values of any variables that appear within it, to distinguish it from an equality which is true under more particular conditions.
   a. Thing
   b. Identity0
   c. Undefined
   d. Undefined

97. An _____ is a function that does not have any effect: it always returns the same value that was used as its argument.
   a. Identity function0
   b. Thing
   c. Undefined
   d. Undefined

98. In statistics, _____ means the most frequent value assumed by a random variable, or occurring in a sampling of a random variable.
   a. Concept
   b. Mode0
   c. Undefined
   d. Undefined

99. In mathematics, the additive inverse, or _____ of a number n is the number that, when added to n, yields zero. The additive inverse of n is denoted −n. For example, 7 is −7, because 7 + (−7) = 0, and the additive inverse of −0.3 is 0.3, because −0.3 + 0.3 = 0.
   a. Thing
   b. Opposite0
   c. Undefined
   d. Undefined

100. In mathematics, the _____ of a number n is the number that, when added to n, yields zero. The _____ of n is denoted −n. For example, 7 is −7, because 7 + (−7) = 0, and the _____ of −0.3 is 0.3, because −0.3 + 0.3 = 0.
   a. Thing
   b. Additive inverse0
   c. Undefined
   d. Undefined

101. In mathematics, defined and _____ are used to explain whether or not expressions have meaningful, sensible, and unambiguous values.
   a. Thing
   b. Undefined0
   c. Undefined
   d. Undefined

102. A _____ is an equation in which each term is either a constant or the product of a constant times the first power of a variable.
   a. Linear equation0
   b. Thing
   c. Undefined
   d. Undefined

103. _____ is a way of expressing a number as a fraction of 100 per cent meaning "per hundred".
   a. Thing
   b. Percent0
   c. Undefined
   d. Undefined

104. A _____ is a function that assigns a number to subsets of a given set.
   a. Thing
   b. Measure0
   c. Undefined
   d. Undefined

105. Compass and straightedge or ruler-and-compass _____ is the _____ of lengths or angles using only an idealized ruler and compass.

a. Thing
b. Construction0
c. Undefined
d. Undefined

106. A _____ is a system of payment named after the small plastic card issued to users of the system.
a. Thing
b. Credit card0
c. Undefined
d. Undefined

107. In mathematics, a _____ or rhodonea curve is a sinusoid plotted in polar coordinates.
a. Rose0
b. Thing
c. Undefined
d. Undefined

108. In banking and accountancy, the outstanding _____ is the amount of money owned, or due, that remains in a deposit account or a loan account at a given date, after all past remittances, payments and withdrawal have been accounted for.
a. Balance0
b. Thing
c. Undefined
d. Undefined

109. _____ is the transport of people on a trip/journey or the process or time involved in a person or object moving from one location to another.
a. Thing
b. Travel0
c. Undefined
d. Undefined

110. Fixed costs are expenses whose total does not change in proportion to the activity of a business.Unit fixed costs decline with volume following a retangular hyperbola as the volume of production.Variable costs by contrast change in relation to the activity of a business such as sales or production volume.Along with variable costs,fixed costs make up one of the two components of total cost. In the most simple production function total cost is equal to fixed costs plus variable costs.In accounting terminology, fixed costs will broadly include all costs which are not included in cost of goods sold, and variable costs are those captured in costs of goods sold. The implicit assumption required to make the equivalence between the accounting and economics terminology is that the accounting period is equal to the period in which fixed costs do not vary in relation to production. In practice, this equivalence does not always hold and depending on the period under consideration by management, some overhead expenses can be adjusted by management, and the specific allocation of each expense to each category will be decided under cost accounting.In business planning and management accounting, usage of the terms fixed costs, variable costs and others will often differ from usage in economics, and may depend on the intended use. For example, costs may be segregated into per unit costs fixed costs per period, and variable costs as a proportion of revenue. Capital expenditures will usually be allocated separately, and depending on the purpose, a portion may be regularly allocated to expenses as depreciation and amortization and seen as a _____ per period, or the entire amount may be considered upfront fixed costs.
a. Thing
b. Fixed cost0
c. Undefined
d. Undefined

111. _____ are expenses whose total does not change in proportion to the activity of a business, within the relevant time period or scale of production
a. Thing
b. Fixed costs0
c. Undefined
d. Undefined

## Chapter 2. Functions, Equations, and Inequalities

112. The existence and properties of _____ are the basis of Euclid's parallel postulate. _____ are two lines on the same plane that do not intersect even assuming that lines extend to infinity in either direction.
   a. Parallel lines0
   b. Thing
   c. Undefined
   d. Undefined

113. In geometry, two lines or planes if one falls on the other in such a way as to create congruent adjacent angles. The term may be used as a noun or adjective. Thus, referring to Figure 1, the line AB is the _____ to CD through the point B.
   a. Thing
   b. Perpendicular0
   c. Undefined
   d. Undefined

114. In mathematics, a _____ is the result of multiplying, or an expression that identifies factors to be multiplied.
   a. Product0
   b. Thing
   c. Undefined
   d. Undefined

115. _____ is a branch of mathematics concerning the study of structure, relation and quantity.
   a. Algebra0
   b. Concept
   c. Undefined
   d. Undefined

116. A _____ is a statement or claimt that a particular event will occur in the future in more certain terms than a forecast.
   a. Prediction0
   b. Thing
   c. Undefined
   d. Undefined

117. In sociology and biology a _____ is the collection of people or organisms of a particular species living in a given geographic area or space, usually measured by a census.
   a. Thing
   b. Population0
   c. Undefined
   d. Undefined

118. A _____, scatter diagram or scatter graph is a graph used in statistics to visually display and relate two quantitative variables of a multidimensional data set by displaying the data as a collection of points, each having one coordinate on a horizontal and one on a vertical axis.
   a. Thing
   b. Scatterplot0
   c. Undefined
   d. Undefined

119. _____ is a mathematical science pertaining to the collection, analysis, interpretation or explanation, and presentation of data. It is applicable to a wide variety of academic disciplines, from the physical and social sciences to the humanities.
   a. Statistics0
   b. Thing
   c. Undefined
   d. Undefined

120. _____ is a regression method that models the relationship between a dependent variable Y, independent variables Xp, and a random term å.
   a. Linear regression0
   b. Thing
   c. Undefined
   d. Undefined

## Chapter 2. Functions, Equations, and Inequalities

121. In probability theory and statistics, _____, also called _____ coefficient, indicates the strength and direction of a linear relationship between two random variables.
    a. Thing
    b. Correlation0
    c. Undefined
    d. Undefined

122. The _____ of a ring $R$ is defined to be the smallest positive integer $n$ such that $n\,a = 0$, for all a in R.
    a. Characteristic0
    b. Thing
    c. Undefined
    d. Undefined

123. _____ is the production of food, feed, fiber, fuel and other goods by the systematic raizing of plants and animals.
    a. Thing
    b. Agriculture0
    c. Undefined
    d. Undefined

124. _____ is a branch of mathematics which deals with triangles, particularly triangles in a plane where one angle of the triangle is 90 degrees, and a variety of other topological relations such as spheres, in other branches, such as spherical _____.
    a. Thing
    b. Trigonometry0
    c. Undefined
    d. Undefined

125. In mathematics, a _____ is a constant multiplicative factor of a certain object. The object can be such things as a variable, a vector, a function, etc. For example, the _____ of $9x^2$ is 9.
    a. Thing
    b. Coefficient0
    c. Undefined
    d. Undefined

126. _____ is a form of periodic payment from an employer to an employee, which is specified in an employment contract.
    a. Gross pay0
    b. Thing
    c. Undefined
    d. Undefined

127. A _____ is a form of periodic payment from an employer to an employee, which is specified in an employment contract.
    a. Salary0
    b. Thing
    c. Undefined
    d. Undefined

128. _____ is a free computer algebra system based on a 1982 version of Macsyma
    a. Maxima0
    b. Thing
    c. Undefined
    d. Undefined

129. _____ are points in the domain of a function at which the function takes a largest value or smallest value, either within a given neighborhood or on the function domain in its entirety.
    a. Thing
    b. Maxima and minima0
    c. Undefined
    d. Undefined

130. In mathematics, maxima and _____, known collectively as extrema, are points in the domain of a function at which the function takes a largest value .

a. Minima0  
b. Thing  
c. Undefined  
d. Undefined

131. _____ is the state of being greater than any finite number, however large.
a. Infinity0  
b. Thing  
c. Undefined  
d. Undefined

132. The _____ is the highest point in a certain portion of a graph.
a. Relative maximum0  
b. Thing  
c. Undefined  
d. Undefined

133. The _____ is the lowest point in a certain portion of a graph.
a. Relative minimum0  
b. Thing  
c. Undefined  
d. Undefined

134. _____ has many meanings, most of which simply .
a. Power0  
b. Thing  
c. Undefined  
d. Undefined

135. _____ is a mathematical subject that includes the study of limits, derivatives, integrals, and power series and constitutes a major part of modern university curriculum.
a. Thing  
b. Calculus0  
c. Undefined  
d. Undefined

136. A _____ is a polynomial function of the form $f(x) = ax^2 + bx + c$, where a, b, c are real numbers and a , 0.
a. Quadratic function0  
b. Event  
c. Undefined  
d. Undefined

137. In geometry and trigonometry, a _____ is defined as an angle between two straight intersecting lines of ninety degrees, or one-quarter of a circle.
a. Right angle0  
b. Thing  
c. Undefined  
d. Undefined

138. In a right triangle, the _____ of the triangle are the two sides that are perpendicular to each other, as opposed to the hypotenuse.
a. Thing  
b. Legs0  
c. Undefined  
d. Undefined

139. The _____ integers are all the integers from zero on upwards.
a. Thing  
b. Nonnegative0  
c. Undefined  
d. Undefined

140. In geometry, a _____ is defined as a quadrilateral where all four of its angles are right angles.
a. Thing  
b. Rectangle0  
c. Undefined  
d. Undefined

## Chapter 2. Functions, Equations, and Inequalities

141. Generally, a _____ is a splitting of something into parts.
   a. Partition0  
   b. Thing  
   c. Undefined  
   d. Undefined

142. _____ is a set, with some particular properties and usually some additional structure, such as the operations of addition or multiplication, for instance.
   a. Space0  
   b. Thing  
   c. Undefined  
   d. Undefined

143. A _____ defined function $f(x)$ of a real variable $x$ is a function whose definition is given differently on disjoint subsets of its domain.
   a. Thing  
   b. Piecewise0  
   c. Undefined  
   d. Undefined

144. _____ are a measure of time.
   a. Thing  
   b. Minutes0  
   c. Undefined  
   d. Undefined

145. In geometry, an _____ of a triangle is a straight line through a vertex and perpendicular to (i.e. forming a right angle with) the opposite side or an extension of the opposite side.
   a. Concept  
   b. Altitude0  
   c. Undefined  
   d. Undefined

146. _____ is the distance around a given two-dimensional object. As a general rule, the _____ of a polygon can always be calculated by adding all the length of the sides together. So, the formula for triangles is P = a + b + c, where a, b and c stand for each side of it. For quadrilaterals the equation is P = a + b + c + d. For equilateral polygons, P = na, where n is the number of sides and a is the side length.
   a. Thing  
   b. Perimeter0  
   c. Undefined  
   d. Undefined

147. In geometry, a _____ (or rhomb; plural rhombi) is a quadrilateral in which all of the sides are of equal length, i.e., it is an equilateral quadrangle.
   a. Rhombus0  
   b. Thing  
   c. Undefined  
   d. Undefined

148. The metre (or _____, see spelling differences) is a measure of length. It is the basic unit of length in the metric system and in the International System of Units (SI), used around the world for general and scientific purposes.
   a. Meter0  
   b. Concept  
   c. Undefined  
   d. Undefined

149. The _____ of a solid object is the three-dimensional concept of how much space it occupies, often quantified numerically.
   a. Volume0  
   b. Thing  
   c. Undefined  
   d. Undefined

## Chapter 2. Functions, Equations, and Inequalities

150. In geometry, _____ angles are angles that have a common ray coming out of the vertex going between two other rays.
   a. Concept
   b. Adjacent0
   c. Undefined
   d. Undefined

151. A _____ is 360° or 2δ radians.
   a. Thing
   b. Turn0
   c. Undefined
   d. Undefined

152. A _____ function is a function for which, intuitively, small changes in the input result in small changes in the output.
   a. Continuous0
   b. Event
   c. Undefined
   d. Undefined

153. In mathematics, a _____ is a quadric surface, with the following equation in Cartesian coordinates: $(x/_a)^2 + (y/_b)^2 = 1$.
   a. Cylinder0
   b. Thing
   c. Undefined
   d. Undefined

154. _____ is a three-dimensional geometric shape formed by straight lines through a fixed point vertex to the points of a fixed curve directrix.
   a. Thing
   b. Right circular cone0
   c. Undefined
   d. Undefined

155. A _____ is a three-dimensional geometric shape formed by straight lines through a fixed point (vertex) to the points of a fixed curve (directrix)
   a. Cone0
   b. Concept
   c. Undefined
   d. Undefined

156. In mathematics, a _____ is the end result of a division problem. It can also be expressed as the number of times the divisor divides into the dividend.
   a. Quotient0
   b. Thing
   c. Undefined
   d. Undefined

157. In mathematics, a _____ of a positive integer n is a way of writing n as a sum of positive integers.
   a. Composition0
   b. Thing
   c. Undefined
   d. Undefined

158. The _____ functions is determined by the nesting of two or more functions to form a single new function.
   a. Thing
   b. Composition of two0
   c. Undefined
   d. Undefined

159. In mathematics, _____ is an elementary arithmetic operation. When one of the numbers is a whole number, _____ is the repeated sum of the other number.

## Chapter 2. Functions, Equations, and Inequalities

a. Thing  
b. Multiplication0  
c. Undefined  
d. Undefined

160. In mathematics, the _____ of two sets A and B is the set that contains all elements of A that also belong to B (or equivalently, all elements of B that also belong to A), but no other elements.  
a. Thing  
b. Intersection0  
c. Undefined  
d. Undefined

161. The function difference divided by the point difference is known as the _____  
a. Thing  
b. Difference quotient0  
c. Undefined  
d. Undefined

162. _____ is, or relates to, the _____ temperature scale .  
a. Celsius0  
b. Thing  
c. Undefined  
d. Undefined

163. _____ is a concept in traditional logic referring to a "type of immediate inference in which from a given proposition another proposition is inferred which has as its subject the predicate of the original proposition and as its predicate the subject of the original proposition (the quality of the proposition being retained)."  
a. Conversion0  
b. Concept  
c. Undefined  
d. Undefined

164. A _____ number is a positive integer which has a positive divisor other than one or itself.  
a. Composite0  
b. Thing  
c. Undefined  
d. Undefined

165. A _____, formed by the composition of one function on another, represents the application of the former to the result of the application of the latter to the argument of the composite.  
a. Thing  
b. Composite function0  
c. Undefined  
d. Undefined

166. _____, from Latin meaning "to make progress", is defined in two different ways. Pure economic _____ is the increase in wealth that an investor has from making an investment, taking into consideration all costs associated with that investment including the opportunity cost of capital.  
a. Profit0  
b. Thing  
c. Undefined  
d. Undefined

167. _____ is a business term for the amount of money that a company receives from its activities in a given period, mostly from sales of products and/or services to customers  
a. Thing  
b. Revenue0  
c. Undefined  
d. Undefined

168. _____ element of an element x with respect to a binary operation * with identity element e is an element y such that x * y = y * x = e. In particular,

## Chapter 2. Functions, Equations, and Inequalities

a. Inverse0  
b. Thing  
c. Undefined  
d. Undefined

169. An _____ is a function which does the reverse of a given function.  
a. Inverse function0  
b. Thing  
c. Undefined  
d. Undefined

170. _____ means "constancy", i.e. if something retains a certain feature even after we change a way of looking at it, then it is symmetric.  
a. Symmetry0  
b. Thing  
c. Undefined  
d. Undefined

171. In mathematics, a _____ in elementary terms is any of a variety of different functions from geometry, such as rotations, reflections and translations.  
a. Thing  
b. Transformation0  
c. Undefined  
d. Undefined

172. In mathematics, a _____ (also spelled reflexion) is a map that transforms an object into its mirror image.  
a. Reflection0  
b. Concept  
c. Undefined  
d. Undefined

173. Equivalence is the condition of being _____ or essentially equal.  
a. Thing  
b. Equivalent0  
c. Undefined  
d. Undefined

174. _____ are functions which satisfy particular symmetry relations, with respect to taking additive inverses.  
a. Even function0  
b. Thing  
c. Undefined  
d. Undefined

175. In mathematics, the multiplicative inverse of a number x, denoted $1/x$ or $x^{-1}$, is the number which, when multiplied by x, yields 1. The multiplicative inverse of x is also called the _____ of x.  
a. Reciprocal0  
b. Thing  
c. Undefined  
d. Undefined

176. In mathematics, a _____ of a number x is a number r such that $r^2 = x$, or in words, a number r whose square (the result of multiplying the number by itself) is x.  
a. Thing  
b. Square root0  
c. Undefined  
d. Undefined

177. In Euclidean geometry, a _____ is moving every point a constant distance in a specified direction.  
a. Translation0  
b. Concept  
c. Undefined  
d. Undefined

178. In mathematics, a _____ is an expression that is constructed from one or more variables and constants, using only the operations of addition, subtraction, multiplication, and constant positive whole number exponents. is a _____. Note in particular that division by an expression containing a variable is not in general allowed in polynomials. [1]

## Chapter 2. Functions, Equations, and Inequalities

a. Thing
c. Undefined
b. Polynomial0
d. Undefined

179. In mathematics, _____ and odd functions are functions which satisfy particular symmetry relations, with respect to taking additive inverses.
   a. Even functions0
   c. Undefined
   b. Thing
   d. Undefined

180. A _____ is a unit of length in the metric system, equal to one thousand metres, the current SI base unit of length
   a. Kilometer0
   c. Undefined
   b. Thing
   d. Undefined

# Chapter 3. Polynomial and Rational Functions

1. In common philosophical language, a proposition or _____, is the content of an assertion, that is, it is true-or-false and defined by the meaning of a particular piece of language.
   - a. Statement0
   - b. Concept
   - c. Undefined
   - d. Undefined

2. An _____ is a combination of numbers, operators, grouping symbols and/or free variables and bound variables arranged in a meaningful way which can be evaluated..
   - a. Thing
   - b. Expression0
   - c. Undefined
   - d. Undefined

3. The word _____ comes from the Latin word linearis, which means created by lines.
   - a. Thing
   - b. Linear0
   - c. Undefined
   - d. Undefined

4. A _____ is an equation in which each term is either a constant or the product of a constant times the first power of a variable.
   - a. Linear equation0
   - b. Thing
   - c. Undefined
   - d. Undefined

5. The mathematical concept of a _____ expresses the intuitive idea of deterministic dependence between two quantities, one of which is viewed as primary and the other as secondary. A _____ then is a way to associate a unique output for each input of a specified type, for example, a real number or an element of a given set.
   - a. Thing
   - b. Function0
   - c. Undefined
   - d. Undefined

6. A _____ is a symbolic representation denoting a quantity or expression. It often represents an "unknown" quantity that has the potential to change.
   - a. Thing
   - b. Variable0
   - c. Undefined
   - d. Undefined

7. A _____ is a set of possible values that a variable can take on in order to satisfy a given set of conditions, which may include equations and inequalities.
   - a. Solution set0
   - b. Thing
   - c. Undefined
   - d. Undefined

8. In mathematics, a _____ may be described informally as a number that can be given by an infinite decimal representation.
   - a. Thing
   - b. Real number0
   - c. Undefined
   - d. Undefined

9. Equivalence is the condition of being _____ or essentially equal.
   - a. Equivalent0
   - b. Thing
   - c. Undefined
   - d. Undefined

10. A _____ signifies a point or points of probability on a subject e.g., the _____ of creativity, which allows for the formation of rule or norm or law by interpretation of the phenomena events that can be created.

## Chapter 3. Polynomial and Rational Functions

a. Principle0  
b. Thing  
c. Undefined  
d. Undefined  

11. In mathematics, _____ is an elementary arithmetic operation. When one of the numbers is a whole number, _____ is the repeated sum of the other number.
    a. Thing
    b. Multiplication0
    c. Undefined
    d. Undefined

12. A _____ is a set of numbers that designate location in a given reference system, such as x,y in a planar _____ system or an x,y,z in a three-dimensional _____ system.
    a. Coordinate0
    b. Thing
    c. Undefined
    d. Undefined

13. _____ are the basic objects of study in graph theory. Informally speaking, a graph is a set of objects called points, nodes, or vertices connected by links called lines or edges.
    a. Thing
    b. Graphs0
    c. Undefined
    d. Undefined

14. In mathematics, the _____ of two sets A and B is the set that contains all elements of A that also belong to B (or equivalently, all elements of B that also belong to A), but no other elements.
    a. Intersection0
    b. Thing
    c. Undefined
    d. Undefined

15. Mathematical _____ is used to represent ideas.
    a. Thing
    b. Notation0
    c. Undefined
    d. Undefined

16. _____ is the writing of numbers in the base-ten numeral system, which uses various symbols called digits for ten distinct values 0, 1, 2, 3, 4, 5, 6, 7, 8 and 9 to represent numbers
    a. Thing
    b. Decimal notation0
    c. Undefined
    d. Undefined

17. _____ forms part of thinking. Considered the most complex of all intellectual functions, _____ has been defined as higher-order cognitive process that requires the modulation and control of more routine or fundamental skills.
    a. Thing
    b. Problem solving0
    c. Undefined
    d. Undefined

18. The _____, the average in everyday English, which is also called the arithmetic _____ (and is distinguished from the geometric _____ or harmonic _____). The average is also called the sample _____. The expected value of a random variable, which is also called the population _____.
    a. Mean0
    b. Thing
    c. Undefined
    d. Undefined

19. A frame of _____ is a particular perspective from which the universe is observed.

## Chapter 3. Polynomial and Rational Functions

a. Thing
c. Undefined
b. Reference0
d. Undefined

20. In mathematics, an _____ is a statement about the relative size or order of two objects.
a. Inequality0
c. Undefined
b. Thing
d. Undefined

21. _____ is a branch of mathematics concerning the study of structure, relation and quantity.
a. Concept
c. Undefined
b. Algebra0
d. Undefined

22. A _____ is a negotiable instrument instructing a financial institution to pay a specific amount of a specific currency from a specific demand account held in the maker/depositor's name with that institution. Both the maker and payee may be natural persons or legal entities.
a. Check0
c. Undefined
b. Thing
d. Undefined

23. Multiple Signal Classification, also known as _____, is an algorithm used for frequency estimation and emitter location.
a. Thing
c. Undefined
b. Music0
d. Undefined

24. In mathematics, an _____, mean, or central tendency of a data set refers to a measure of the "middle" or "expected" value of the data set.
a. Average0
c. Undefined
b. Concept
d. Undefined

25. A _____ is a special kind of ratio, indicating a relationship between two measurements with different units, such as miles to gallons or cents to pounds.
a. Rate0
c. Undefined
b. Thing
d. Undefined

26. In mathematics, a _____ is a two-dimensional manifold or surface that is perfectly flat.
a. Plane0
c. Undefined
b. Thing
d. Undefined

27. In mathematics, _____ are two-dimensional manifolds or surfaces that are perfectly flat.
a. Thing
c. Undefined
b. Planes0
d. Undefined

28. _____ is the process of reducing the number of significant digits in a number.
a. Concept
c. Undefined
b. Rounding0
d. Undefined

29. In mathematics, and in particular in abstract algebra, the _____ is a property of binary operations that generalises the distributive law from elementary algebra.

a. Distributive property0  
b. Thing  
c. Undefined  
d. Undefined

30. _____ is the transport of people on a trip/journey or the process or time involved in a person or object moving from one location to another.
a. Thing  
b. Travel0  
c. Undefined  
d. Undefined

31. A _____ is a type of debt. All material things can be lent but this article focuses exclusively on monetary loans. Like all debt instruments, a _____ entails the redistribution of financial assets over time, between the lender and the borrower.
a. Loan0  
b. Thing  
c. Undefined  
d. Undefined

32. _____ is a kind of property which exists as magnitude or multitude. It is among the basic classes of things along with quality, substance, change, and relation.
a. Thing  
b. Amount0  
c. Undefined  
d. Undefined

33. _____ is the fee paid on borrowed money.
a. Interest0  
b. Thing  
c. Undefined  
d. Undefined

34. _____ or investing is a term with several closely-related meanings in business management, finance and economics, related to saving or deferring consumption.
a. Thing  
b. Investment0  
c. Undefined  
d. Undefined

35. An _____ is the fee paid on borrow money.
a. Interest rate0  
b. Concept  
c. Undefined  
d. Undefined

36. In mathematics, an inequality is a statement about the relative size or order of two objects. For example 14 > 10, or 14 is _____ 10.
a. Thing  
b. Greater than0  
c. Undefined  
d. Undefined

37. _____ is the distance around a given two-dimensional object. As a general rule, the _____ of a polygon can always be calculated by adding all the length of the sides together. So, the formula for triangles is P = a + b + c, where a, b and c stand for each side of it. For quadrilaterals the equation is P = a + b + c + d. For equilateral polygons, P = na, where n is the number of sides and a is the side length.
a. Thing  
b. Perimeter0  
c. Undefined  
d. Undefined

## Chapter 3. Polynomial and Rational Functions

38. A _____ is a unit of length, usually used to measure distance, in a number of different systems, including Imperial units, United States customary units and Norwegian/Swedish mil. Its size can vary from system to system, but in each is between 1 and 10 kilometers. In contemporary English contexts _____ refers to either:
   a. Mile0
   b. Thing
   c. Undefined
   d. Undefined

39. A _____ is a first degree polynomial mathematical function of the form: $f(x) = mx + b$ where m and b are real constants and x is a real variable.
   a. Thing
   b. Linear function0
   c. Undefined
   d. Undefined

40. In mathematics and the mathematical sciences, a _____ is a fixed, but possibly unspecified, value. This is in contrast to a variable, which is not fixed.
   a. Thing
   b. Constant0
   c. Undefined
   d. Undefined

41. In geographic information systems, a _____ comprises an entity with a geographic location, typically determined by points, arcs, or polygons. Carriageways and cadastres exemplify _____ data.
   a. Thing
   b. Feature0
   c. Undefined
   d. Undefined

42. In geometry, a _____ is defined as a quadrilateral where all four of its angles are right angles.
   a. Thing
   b. Rectangle0
   c. Undefined
   d. Undefined

43. _____, from Latin meaning "to make progress", is defined in two different ways. Pure economic _____ is the increase in wealth that an investor has from making an investment, taking into consideration all costs associated with that investment including the opportunity cost of capital.
   a. Thing
   b. Profit0
   c. Undefined
   d. Undefined

44. Initial objects are also called _____, and terminal objects are also called final.
   a. Thing
   b. Coterminal0
   c. Undefined
   d. Undefined

45. A _____ is an individual or household that purchases and uses goods and services generated within the economy.
   a. Thing
   b. Consumer0
   c. Undefined
   d. Undefined

46. _____ is a form of periodic payment from an employer to an employee, which is specified in an employment contract.
   a. Thing
   b. Gross pay0
   c. Undefined
   d. Undefined

## Chapter 3. Polynomial and Rational Functions 39

47. The payment of _____ as remuneration for services rendered or products sold is a common way to reward sales people.
   a. Commission0
   b. Thing
   c. Undefined
   d. Undefined

48. A _____ is a form of periodic payment from an employer to an employee, which is specified in an employment contract.
   a. Thing
   b. Salary0
   c. Undefined
   d. Undefined

49. A _____ is one of the basic shapes of geometry: a polygon with three vertices and three sides which are straight line segments.
   a. Triangle0
   b. Thing
   c. Undefined
   d. Undefined

50. A _____ is a function that assigns a number to subsets of a given set.
   a. Thing
   b. Measure0
   c. Undefined
   d. Undefined

51. _____ is an adjective usually refering to being in the centre.
   a. Thing
   b. Central0
   c. Undefined
   d. Undefined

52. In botany, _____ are above-ground plant organs specialized for photosynthesis. Their characteristics are typically analyzed by using Fiobonacci's sequences.
   a. Thing
   b. Leaves0
   c. Undefined
   d. Undefined

53. _____ is the level of functional and/or metabolic efficiency of an organism at both the micro level.
   a. Health0
   b. Thing
   c. Undefined
   d. Undefined

54. A _____ is a quadrilateral, which is defined as a shape with four sides, which has a pair of parallel sides.
   a. Thing
   b. Trapezoid0
   c. Undefined
   d. Undefined

55. The _____ of a solid object is the three-dimensional concept of how much space it occupies, often quantified numerically.
   a. Volume0
   b. Thing
   c. Undefined
   d. Undefined

56. In Euclidean geometry, a _____ is the set of all points in a plane at a fixed distance, called the radius, from a given point, the center.
   a. Circle0
   b. Thing
   c. Undefined
   d. Undefined

## Chapter 3. Polynomial and Rational Functions

57. _____ is a concept in traditional logic referring to a "type of immediate inference in which from a given proposition another proposition is inferred which has as its subject the predicate of the original proposition and as its predicate the subject of the original proposition (the quality of the proposition being retained)."
   a. Conversion0
   b. Concept
   c. Undefined
   d. Undefined

58. In mathematics, a _____ is the set of all points in three-dimensional space ($R^3$) which are at distance r from a fixed point of that space, where r is a positive real number called the radius of the _____. The fixed point is called the center or centre, and is not part of the _____ itself.
   a. Thing
   b. Sphere0
   c. Undefined
   d. Undefined

59. _____ is a physical property of a system that underlies the common notions of hot and cold; something that is hotter has the greater _____.
   a. Temperature0
   b. Thing
   c. Undefined
   d. Undefined

60. _____ is a temperature scale named after the German physicist Daniel Gabriel _____ , who proposed it in 1724.
   a. Fahrenheit0
   b. Thing
   c. Undefined
   d. Undefined

61. _____ is, or relates to, the _____ temperature scale .
   a. Celsius0
   b. Thing
   c. Undefined
   d. Undefined

62. _____ is a way of expressing a number as a fraction of 100 per cent meaning "per hundred".
   a. Thing
   b. Percent0
   c. Undefined
   d. Undefined

63. A _____ is a number that is less than zero.
   a. Negative number0
   b. Thing
   c. Undefined
   d. Undefined

64. In plane geometry, a _____ is a polygon with four equal sides, four right angles, and parallel opposite sides. In algebra, the _____ of a number is that number multiplied by itself.
   a. Thing
   b. Square0
   c. Undefined
   d. Undefined

65. In mathematics, a _____ of a number x is a number r such that $r^2$ = x, or in words, a number r whose square (the result of multiplying the number by itself) is x.
   a. Square root0
   b. Thing
   c. Undefined
   d. Undefined

66. In mathematics, a _____ of a complex-valued function f is a member x of the domain of f such that f(x) vanishes at x, that is, x : f (x) = 0.

## Chapter 3. Polynomial and Rational Functions

a. Thing  
b. Root0  
c. Undefined  
d. Undefined

67. _____ is the symbol used to indicate the nth root of a number
    a. Thing
    b. Radical0
    c. Undefined
    d. Undefined

68. In mathematics, a _____ is a number in the form of a + bi where a and b are real numbers, and i is the imaginary unit, with the property i 2 = −1. The real number a is called the real part of the _____, and the real number b is the imaginary part.
    a. Complex number0
    b. Thing
    c. Undefined
    d. Undefined

69. In mathematics, the _____ of a complex number z, is the first element of the ordered pair of real numbers representing z, i.e. if z = (x,y), or equivalently, z = x + iy, then the _____ of z is x. It is denoted by Re{z} . The complex function which maps z to the _____ of z is not holomorphic.
    a. Real part0
    b. Thing
    c. Undefined
    d. Undefined

70. In mathematics, an _____ number is a complex number whose square is a negative real number. They were defined in 1572 by Rafael Bombelli.
    a. Imaginary0
    b. Thing
    c. Undefined
    d. Undefined

71. In mathematics, the _____ of a complex number z, is the second element of the ordered pair of real numbers representing z, i.e. if z = (x,y), or equivalently, z = x + iy, then the _____ of z is y.
    a. Imaginary part0
    b. Thing
    c. Undefined
    d. Undefined

72. In mathematics, an _____ is a complex number whose square is a negative real number. They were defined in 1572 by Rafael Bombelli.
    a. Thing
    b. Imaginary number0
    c. Undefined
    d. Undefined

73. In statistics, _____ means the most frequent value assumed by a random variable, or occurring in a sampling of a random variable.
    a. Concept
    b. Mode0
    c. Undefined
    d. Undefined

74. The _____ relates to the binary operation of multiplication and addition.
    a. Thing
    b. Distributive law0
    c. Undefined
    d. Undefined

75. In algebra, a _____ is a binomial formed by taking the opposite of the second term of a binomial.

a. Conjugate0  
b. Thing  
c. Undefined  
d. Undefined

76. In mathematics, a _____ is the result of multiplying, or an expression that identifies factors to be multiplied.
   a. Product0
   b. Thing
   c. Undefined
   d. Undefined

77. A _____ is the part of a fraction that tells how many equal parts make up a whole, and which is used in the name of the fraction: "halves", "thirds", "fourths" or "quarters", "fifths" and so on.
   a. Concept
   b. Denominator0
   c. Undefined
   d. Undefined

78. In mathematics, a _____ of an integer n, also called a factor of n, is an integer which evenly divides n without leaving a remainder.
   a. Divisor0
   b. Thing
   c. Undefined
   d. Undefined

79. In mathematics, a _____ is the end result of a division problem. It can also be expressed as the number of times the divisor divides into the dividend.
   a. Thing
   b. Quotient0
   c. Undefined
   d. Undefined

80. A _____ is the result of the addition of a set of numbers. The numbers may be natural numbers, complex numbers, matrices, or still more complicated objects. An infinite _____ is a subtle procedure known as a series.
   a. Thing
   b. Sum0
   c. Undefined
   d. Undefined

81. In mathematics, a _____ is a polynomial equation of the second degree. The general form is $ax^2 + bx + c = 0$.
   a. Thing
   b. Quadratic equation0
   c. Undefined
   d. Undefined

82. A _____ is a polynomial function of the form $f(x) = ax^2 + bx + c$, where a, b, c are real numbers and a , 0.
   a. Quadratic function0
   b. Event
   c. Undefined
   d. Undefined

83. _____ is a notation for writing numbers that is often used by scientists and mathematicians to make it easier to write large and small numbers.
   a. Thing
   b. Scientific notation0
   c. Undefined
   d. Undefined

84. In mathematics, _____ is the decomposition of an object into a product of other objects, or factors, which when multiplied together give the original.
   a. Factoring0
   b. Thing
   c. Undefined
   d. Undefined

## Chapter 3. Polynomial and Rational Functions

85. _____ is a technique used in algebra to solve quadratic equations, in analytic geometry for determining the shapes of graphs, and in calculus for computing integrals, including, but hardly limited to, the integrals that define Laplace transforms. The essential objective is to reduce a quadratic polynomial in a variable in an equation or expression to a squared polynomial of linear order. This can reduce an equation or integral to one that is more easily solved or evaluated.
    a. Thing
    b. Completing the square0
    c. Undefined
    d. Undefined

86. The term _____ can refer to an integer which is the square of some other integer, or an algebraic expression that can be factored as the square of some other expression.
    a. Perfect square0
    b. Thing
    c. Undefined
    d. Undefined

87. In mathematics, a _____ is a constant multiplicative factor of a certain object. The object can be such things as a variable, a vector, a function, etc. For example, the _____ of $9x^2$ is 9.
    a. Coefficient0
    b. Thing
    c. Undefined
    d. Undefined

88. In mathematics, _____ expressions is used to reduce the expression into the lowest possible term.
    a. Simplifying0
    b. Thing
    c. Undefined
    d. Undefined

89. The _____ is a method of finding the derivative of a function that is the quotient of two other functions for which derivatives exist.
    a. Quotient rule0
    b. Thing
    c. Undefined
    d. Undefined

90. In mathematics, _____ are used to indicate the square root of a number.
    a. Radicals0
    b. Thing
    c. Undefined
    d. Undefined

91. In elementary algebra, a _____ is a polynomial with two terms: the sum of two monomials. It is the simplest kind of polynomial except for a monomial.
    a. Binomial0
    b. Thing
    c. Undefined
    d. Undefined

92. A quadratic equation with real solutions, called roots, which may be real or complex, is given by the _____: $x = {-b \pm \sqrt{b^2 - 4ac}}/{2a}$.
    a. Thing
    b. Quadratic formula0
    c. Undefined
    d. Undefined

93. The plus and _____ signs are mathematical symbols used to represent the notions of positive and negative as well as the operations of addition and subtraction.
    a. Thing
    b. Minus0
    c. Undefined
    d. Undefined

## Chapter 3. Polynomial and Rational Functions

94. _____ of a polynomial with real or complex coefficients is a certain expression in the coefficients of the polynomial which is equal to zero if and only if the polynomial has a multiple root i.e. a root with multiplicity greater than one in the complex numbers.
   a. Discriminant0
   b. Thing
   c. Undefined
   d. Undefined

95. Any point where a graph makes contact with an coordinate axis is called an _____ of the graph
   a. Intercept0
   b. Thing
   c. Undefined
   d. Undefined

96. _____ is a mathematical science pertaining to the collection, analysis, interpretation or explanation, and presentation of data. It is applicable to a wide variety of academic disciplines, from the physical and social sciences to the humanities.
   a. Statistics0
   b. Thing
   c. Undefined
   d. Undefined

97. A _____ can refer to a line joining two nonadjacent vertices of a polygon or polyhedron, or in some contexts any upward or downward sloping line. .
   a. Diagonal0
   b. Thing
   c. Undefined
   d. Undefined

98. _____ has one 90° internal angle a right angle.
   a. Right triangle0
   b. Thing
   c. Undefined
   d. Undefined

99. In mathematics, there are several meanings of _____ depending on the subject.
   a. Thing
   b. Degree0
   c. Undefined
   d. Undefined

100. In geometry, the _____ of an object is a point in some sense in the middle of the object.
   a. Center0
   b. Thing
   c. Undefined
   d. Undefined

101. In mathematics, the _____ of a coordinate system is the point where the axes of the system intersect.
   a. Thing
   b. Origin0
   c. Undefined
   d. Undefined

102. In geometry, a _____ is a special kind of point, usually a corner of a polygon, polyhedron, or higher dimensional polytope. In the geometry of curves a _____ is a point of where the first derivative of curvature is zero. In graph theory, a _____ is the fundamental unit out of which graphs are formed
   a. Thing
   b. Vertex0
   c. Undefined
   d. Undefined

103. _____ means "constancy", i.e. if something retains a certain feature even after we change a way of looking at it, then it is symmetric.

## Chapter 3. Polynomial and Rational Functions

a. Symmetry0  
c. Undefined  
b. Thing  
d. Undefined

104. An _____ is a straight line around which a geometric figure can be rotated.
a. Axis0  
c. Undefined  
b. Thing  
d. Undefined

105. _____ of a two-dimensional figure is a line such that, if a perpendicular is constructed, any two points lying on the perpendicular at equal distances from the _____ are identical.
a. Axis of symmetry0  
c. Undefined  
b. Thing  
d. Undefined

106. In mathematics, the _____ is a conic section generated by the intersection of a right circular conical surface and a plane parallel to a generating straight line of that surface. It can also be defined as locus of points in a plane which are equidistant from a given point.
a. Thing  
c. Undefined  
b. Parabola0  
d. Undefined

107. In mathematics, a _____ in elementary terms is any of a variety of different functions from geometry, such as rotations, reflections and translations.
a. Thing  
c. Undefined  
b. Transformation0  
d. Undefined

108. In Euclidean geometry, a _____ is moving every point a constant distance in a specified direction.
a. Translation0  
c. Undefined  
b. Concept  
d. Undefined

109. In mathematics, a _____ (also spelled reflexion) is a map that transforms an object into its mirror image.
a. Reflection0  
c. Undefined  
b. Concept  
d. Undefined

110. A _____ is 360° or 2δ radians.
a. Thing  
c. Undefined  
b. Turn0  
d. Undefined

111. An _____ is a collection of two not necessarily distinct objects, one of which is distinguished as the first coordinate and the other as the second coordinate.
a. Ordered pair0  
c. Undefined  
b. Thing  
d. Undefined

112. The _____ of measurement are a globally standardized and modernized form of the metric system.
a. Thing  
c. Undefined  
b. Units0  
d. Undefined

113. The _____ of a ring $R$ is defined to be the smallest positive integer $n$ such that $n$ a = 0, for all a in R.

# Chapter 3. Polynomial and Rational Functions

a. Thing  
c. Undefined  
b. Characteristic0  
d. Undefined

114. In mathematics, the _____ of a function is the set of all "output" values produced by that function. Given a function $f : A \to B$, the _____ of $f$, is defined to be the set $\{x \in B : x = f(a) \text{ for some } a \in A\}$.
   a. Range0  
   b. Thing  
   c. Undefined  
   d. Undefined

115. In elementary algebra, an _____ is a set that contains every real number between two indicated numbers and may contain the two numbers themselves.
   a. Interval0  
   b. Thing  
   c. Undefined  
   d. Undefined

116. In combinatorial mathematics, a _____ is an un-ordered collection of unique elements.
   a. Combination0  
   b. Concept  
   c. Undefined  
   d. Undefined

117. _____ of an object is its speed in a particular direction.
   a. Velocity0  
   b. Thing  
   c. Undefined  
   d. Undefined

118. A _____ is a vehicle, missile or aircraft which obtains thrust by the reaction to the ejection of fast moving fluid from within a _____ engine.
   a. Rocket0  
   b. Thing  
   c. Undefined  
   d. Undefined

119. _____, Greek for "knowledge of nature," is the branch of science concerned with the discovery and characterization of universal laws which govern matter, energy, space, and time.
   a. Physics0  
   b. Thing  
   c. Undefined  
   d. Undefined

120. A _____ is any object propelled through space by the applicationp of a force.
   a. Projectile0  
   b. Thing  
   c. Undefined  
   d. Undefined

121. _____ is the application of tools and a processing medium to the transformation of raw materials into finished goods for sale.
   a. Thing  
   b. Manufacturing0  
   c. Undefined  
   d. Undefined

122. A _____ is a four-sided plane figure that has two sets of opposite parallel sides.
   a. Concept  
   b. Parallelogram0  
   c. Undefined  
   d. Undefined

123. _____ is a business term for the amount of money that a company receives from its activities in a given period, mostly from sales of products and/or services to customers

## Chapter 3. Polynomial and Rational Functions

a. Revenue0  
b. Thing  
c. Undefined  
d. Undefined  

124. In geometry, _____ angles are angles that have a common ray coming out of the vertex going between two other rays.
a. Adjacent0  
b. Concept  
c. Undefined  
d. Undefined  

125. The function difference divided by the point difference is known as the _____
a. Difference quotient0  
b. Thing  
c. Undefined  
d. Undefined  

126. In mathematics, a _____ number is a number which can be expressed as a ratio of two integers. Non-integer _____ numbers (commonly called fractions) are usually written as the vulgar fraction a / b, where b is not zero.
a. Rational0  
b. Thing  
c. Undefined  
d. Undefined  

127. In statistics, a _____ measure is one which is measuring what is supposed to measure.
a. Thing  
b. Valid0  
c. Undefined  
d. Undefined  

128. The _____ is the number or expression underneath the radical sign.
a. Thing  
b. Radicand0  
c. Undefined  
d. Undefined  

129. _____ has many meanings, most of which simply .
a. Thing  
b. Power0  
c. Undefined  
d. Undefined  

130. In mathematics, a _____ of a k-place relation $L \subseteq X_1 \times ... \times X_k$ is one of the sets $X_j$, $1 \leq j \leq k$. In the special case where k = 2 and $L \subseteq X_1 \times X_2$ is a function $L : X_1 \to X_2$, it is conventional to refer to $X_1$ as the _____ of the function and to refer to $X_2$ as the codomain of the function.
a. Domain0  
b. Thing  
c. Undefined  
d. Undefined  

131. Acid _____ ratio measures the ability of a company to use its near cash or quick assets to immediately extinguish its current liabilities.
a. Test0  
b. Thing  
c. Undefined  
d. Undefined  

132. A _____ is a one-dimensional picture in which the integers are shown as specially-marked points evenly spaced on a line.
a. Number line0  
b. Thing  
c. Undefined  
d. Undefined  

133. In mathematics, the _____ (or modulus) of a real number is its numerical value without regard to its sign.

## Chapter 3. Polynomial and Rational Functions

a. Thing
c. Undefined
b. Absolute value0
d. Undefined

134. In mathematics and more specifically set theory, the _____ set is the unique set which contains no elements.
a. Thing
c. Undefined
b. Empty0
d. Undefined

135. _____ interest refers to the fact that whenever interest is calculated, it is based not only on the original principal, but also on any unpaid interest that has been added to the principal.
a. Thing
c. Undefined
b. Compound0
d. Undefined

136. _____ refers to the fact that whenever interest is calculated, it is based not only on the original principal, but also on any unpaid interest that has been added to the principal. The more frequently interest is compounded, the faster the balance grows.
a. Compound interest0
c. Undefined
b. Concept
d. Undefined

137. _____ is the production of food, feed, fiber, fuel and other goods by the systematic raizing of plants and animals.
a. Agriculture0
c. Undefined
b. Thing
d. Undefined

138. In mathematics, a _____ is a countable collection of open covers of a topological space that satisfies certain separation axioms.
a. Thing
c. Undefined
b. Development0
d. Undefined

139. In logic and mathematics, logical _____ (usual symbol and) is a two-place logical operation that results in a value of true if both of its operands are true, otherwise a value of false.
a. Conjunction0
c. Undefined
b. Concept
d. Undefined

140. In geometry, a line _____ is a part of a line that is bounded by two end points, and contains every point on the line between its end points.
a. Concept
c. Undefined
b. Segment0
d. Undefined

141. In geometry, an _____ is a point at which a line segment or ray terminates.
a. Thing
c. Undefined
b. Endpoint0
d. Undefined

142. In logic and mathematics, logical _____ (written or) is a logical operator that results in true just whenever some of its operands are true.
a. Disjunction0
c. Undefined
b. Thing
d. Undefined

## Chapter 3. Polynomial and Rational Functions

143. _____ is the notation in which permitted values for a variable are expressed as ranging over a certain interval; "5 < x < 9" is an example of the application of _____.
 a. Interval notation0
 b. Thing
 c. Undefined
 d. Undefined

144. In astronomy, geography, geometry and related sciences and contexts, a plane is said to be _____ at a given point if it is locally perpendicular to the gradient of the gravity field, i.e., with the direction of the gravitational force at that point.
 a. Thing
 b. Horizontal0
 c. Undefined
 d. Undefined

145. In geometry, two lines or planes if one falls on the other in such a way as to create congruent adjacent angles. The term may be used as a noun or adjective. Thus, referring to Figure 1, the line AB is the _____ to CD through the point B.
 a. Thing
 b. Perpendicular0
 c. Undefined
 d. Undefined

146. _____ is the middle point of a line segment.
 a. Thing
 b. Midpoint0
 c. Undefined
 d. Undefined

147. _____ is often used to describe the measurement of the steepness, incline, gradient, or grade of a straight line. The _____ is defined as the ratio of the "rise" divided by the "run" between two points on a line, or in other words, the ratio of the altitude change to the horizontal distance between any two points on the line.
 a. Slope0
 b. Thing
 c. Undefined
 d. Undefined

148. In a right triangle, the _____ of the triangle are the two sides that are perpendicular to each other, as opposed to the hypotenuse.
 a. Thing
 b. Legs0
 c. Undefined
 d. Undefined

149. In geometry and trigonometry, a _____ is defined as an angle between two straight intersecting lines of ninety degrees, or one-quarter of a circle.
 a. Right angle0
 b. Thing
 c. Undefined
 d. Undefined

150. A _____ are accounts maintained by commercial banks, savings and loan associations, credit unions, and mutual savings banks that pay interest but can not be used directly as money by, for example, writing a cheque.
 a. Thing
 b. Savings account0
 c. Undefined
 d. Undefined

151. _____, in economics and political economy, are the distributions or payments awarded to the various suppliers of the factors of production.
 a. Returns0
 b. Thing
 c. Undefined
 d. Undefined

## Chapter 4. Exponential and Logarithmic Functions

1. In mathematics and elsewhere, the adjective _____ means fourth order, such as the function x4. A _____ number is a number which equals the fourth power of an integer.
   a. Thing
   b. Quartic0
   c. Undefined
   d. Undefined

2. A _____ is a polynomial function with a degree of four. It has the same limit when the argument goes to positive or negative infinity.
   a. Quartic function0
   b. Thing
   c. Undefined
   d. Undefined

3. In mathematics, a _____ number is a number which can be expressed as a ratio of two integers. Non-integer _____ numbers (commonly called fractions) are usually written as the vulgar fraction a / b, where b is not zero.
   a. Thing
   b. Rational0
   c. Undefined
   d. Undefined

4. In mathematics, a _____ is any function which can be written as the ratio of two polynomial functions.
   a. Thing
   b. Rational function0
   c. Undefined
   d. Undefined

5. In mathematics, a _____ is an expression that is constructed from one or more variables and constants, using only the operations of addition, subtraction, multiplication, and constant positive whole number exponents. is a _____. Note in particular that division by an expression containing a variable is not in general allowed in polynomials. [1]
   a. Polynomial0
   b. Thing
   c. Undefined
   d. Undefined

6. The mathematical concept of a _____ expresses the intuitive idea of deterministic dependence between two quantities, one of which is viewed as primary and the other as secondary. A _____ then is a way to associate a unique output for each input of a specified type, for example, a real number or an element of a given set.
   a. Thing
   b. Function0
   c. Undefined
   d. Undefined

7. In mathematics, a _____ may be described informally as a number that can be given by an infinite decimal representation.
   a. Real number0
   b. Thing
   c. Undefined
   d. Undefined

8. In mathematics, a _____ can mean either an element of the set {1, 2, 3, ...} (i.e the positive integers) or an element of the set {0, 1, 2, 3, ...} (i.e. the non-negative integers).
   a. Whole number0
   b. Concept
   c. Undefined
   d. Undefined

9. In mathematics, a _____ is a constant multiplicative factor of a certain object. The object can be such things as a variable, a vector, a function, etc. For example, the _____ of $9x^2$ is 9.
   a. Thing
   b. Coefficient0
   c. Undefined
   d. Undefined

10. _____ is a mathematical operation, written $a^n$, involving two numbers, the base a and the exponent n.

## Chapter 4. Exponential and Logarithmic Functions

a. Thing  
b. Exponentiating0  
c. Undefined  
d. Undefined

11. _____ is a mathematical operation, written $a^n$, involving two numbers, the base a and the exponent n.  
a. Exponentiation0  
b. Thing  
c. Undefined  
d. Undefined

12. The _____ of a ring R is defined to be the smallest positive integer n such that n a = 0, for all a in R.  
a. Characteristic0  
b. Thing  
c. Undefined  
d. Undefined

13. _____ are the basic objects of study in graph theory. Informally speaking, a graph is a set of objects called points, nodes, or vertices connected by links called lines or edges.  
a. Thing  
b. Graphs0  
c. Undefined  
d. Undefined

14. In mathematics, the _____ of a function is the set of all "output" values produced by that function. Given a function $f: A \to B$, the _____ of $f$, is defined to be the set $\{x \in B : x = f(a) \text{ for some } a \in A\}$.  
a. Range0  
b. Thing  
c. Undefined  
d. Undefined

15. The _____ is the highest point in a certain portion of a graph.  
a. Thing  
b. Relative maximum0  
c. Undefined  
d. Undefined

16. The _____ is the lowest point in a certain portion of a graph.  
a. Relative minimum0  
b. Thing  
c. Undefined  
d. Undefined

17. In mathematics, a _____ of a k-place relation $L \subseteq X_1 \times \ldots \times X_k$ is one of the sets $X_j$, $1 \leq j \leq k$. In the special case where k = 2 and $L \subseteq X_1 \times X_2$ is a function $L : X_1 \to X_2$, it is conventional to refer to $X_1$ as the _____ of the function and to refer to $X_2$ as the codomain of the function.  
a. Domain0  
b. Thing  
c. Undefined  
d. Undefined

18. A _____ function is a function for which, intuitively, small changes in the input result in small changes in the output.  
a. Continuous0  
b. Event  
c. Undefined  
d. Undefined

19. Acid _____ ratio measures the ability of a company to use its near cash or quick assets to immediately extinguish its current liabilities.  
a. Thing  
b. Test0  
c. Undefined  
d. Undefined

20. In mathematics, a _____ is the result of multiplying, or an expression that identifies factors to be multiplied.

## Chapter 4. Exponential and Logarithmic Functions

a. Product0  
b. Thing  
c. Undefined  
d. Undefined  

21. In mathematics, factorization (British English: factorisation) or factoring is the decomposition of an object (for example, a number, a polynomial, or a matrix) into a product of other objects, or _____, which when multiplied together give the original.
    a. Thing  
    b. Factors0  
    c. Undefined  
    d. Undefined  

22. The word _____ comes from the Latin word linearis, which means created by lines.
    a. Thing  
    b. Linear0  
    c. Undefined  
    d. Undefined  

23. A _____ signifies a point or points of probability on a subject e.g., the _____ of creativity, which allows for the formation of rule or norm or law by interpretation of the phenomena events that can be created.
    a. Principle0  
    b. Thing  
    c. Undefined  
    d. Undefined  

24. The _____ of a member of a multiset is how many memberships in the multiset it has.
    a. Multiplicity0  
    b. Thing  
    c. Undefined  
    d. Undefined  

25. In abstract algebra, _____ consists of sets with binary operations that satisfy certain axioms.
    a. Thing  
    b. Grouping0  
    c. Undefined  
    d. Undefined  

26. In trigonometry, the _____ is a function defined as $\tan x = \sin x / \cos x$. The function is so-named because it can be defined as the length of a certain segment of a _____ (in the geometric sense) to the unit circle. In plane geometry, a line is _____ to a curve, at some point, if both line and curve pass through the point with the same direction.
    a. Tangent0  
    b. Thing  
    c. Undefined  
    d. Undefined  

27. In mathematics, _____ is the decomposition of an object into a product of other objects, or factors, which when multiplied together give the original.
    a. Factoring0  
    b. Thing  
    c. Undefined  
    d. Undefined  

28. In mathematics, there are several meanings of _____ depending on the subject.
    a. Degree0  
    b. Thing  
    c. Undefined  
    d. Undefined  

29. A _____ is a set of numbers that designate location in a given reference system, such as x,y in a planar _____ system or an x,y,z in a three-dimensional _____ system.
    a. Coordinate0  
    b. Thing  
    c. Undefined  
    d. Undefined

## Chapter 4. Exponential and Logarithmic Functions

30. In elementary algebra, an _____ is a set that contains every real number between two indicated numbers and may contain the two numbers themselves.
   a. Thing
   b. Interval0
   c. Undefined
   d. Undefined

31. A _____ is a negotiable instrument instructing a financial institution to pay a specific amount of a specific currency from a specific demand account held in the maker/depositor's name with that institution. Both the maker and payee may be natural persons or legal entities.
   a. Check0
   b. Thing
   c. Undefined
   d. Undefined

32. In plane geometry, a _____ is a polygon with four equal sides, four right angles, and parallel opposite sides. In algebra, the _____ of a number is that number multiplied by itself.
   a. Thing
   b. Square0
   c. Undefined
   d. Undefined

33. _____ the expected value of a random variable displays the average or central value of the variable. It is a summary value of the distribution of the variable.
   a. Thing
   b. Determining0
   c. Undefined
   d. Undefined

34. In mathematics, a _____ is a statement that can be proved on the basis of explicitly stated or previously agreed assumptions.
   a. Theorem0
   b. Thing
   c. Undefined
   d. Undefined

35. The _____ implies that on any great circle around the world, the temperature, pressure, elevation, carbon dioxide concentration, or anything else that varies continuously, there will always exist two antipodal points that share the same value for that variable.
   a. Intermediate Value Theorem0
   b. Thing
   c. Undefined
   d. Undefined

36. In mathematics, the concept of a _____ tries to capture the intuitive idea of a geometrical one-dimensional and continuous object. A simple example is the circle.
   a. Thing
   b. Curve0
   c. Undefined
   d. Undefined

37. In mathematics, the additive inverse, or _____ of a number n is the number that, when added to n, yields zero. The additive inverse of n is denoted −n. For example, 7 is −7, because 7 + (−7) = 0, and the additive inverse of −0.3 is 0.3, because −0.3 + 0.3 = 0.
   a. Opposite0
   b. Thing
   c. Undefined
   d. Undefined

38. In mathematics, the _____ of a number n is the number that, when added to n, yields zero. The _____ of n is denoted −n. For example, 7 is −7, because 7 + (−7) = 0, and the _____ of −0.3 is 0.3, because −0.3 + 0.3 = 0.

## 54 Chapter 4. Exponential and Logarithmic Functions

a. Thing
c. Undefined
b. Additive inverse0
d. Undefined

39. _____ is the design, analysis, and/or construction of works for practical purposes.
a. Thing
c. Undefined
b. Engineering0
d. Undefined

40. In business, particularly accounting, a _____ is the time intervals that the accounts, statement, payments, or other calculations cover.
a. Thing
c. Undefined
b. Period0
d. Undefined

41. In geographic information systems, a _____ comprises an entity with a geographic location, typically determined by points, arcs, or polygons. Carriageways and cadastres exemplify _____ data.
a. Thing
c. Undefined
b. Feature0
d. Undefined

42. Initial objects are also called _____, and terminal objects are also called final.
a. Coterminal0
c. Undefined
b. Thing
d. Undefined

43. _____ is a synonym for information.
a. Data0
c. Undefined
b. Thing
d. Undefined

44. A _____ is a first degree polynomial mathematical function of the form: $f(x) = mx + b$ where m and b are real constants and x is a real variable.
a. Linear function0
c. Undefined
b. Thing
d. Undefined

45. Mathematical _____ is used to represent ideas.
a. Notation0
c. Undefined
b. Thing
d. Undefined

46. _____ is the writing of numbers in the base-ten numeral system, which uses various symbols called digits for ten distinct values 0, 1, 2, 3, 4, 5, 6, 7, 8 and 9 to represent numbers
a. Thing
c. Undefined
b. Decimal notation0
d. Undefined

47. A _____, scatter diagram or scatter graph is a graph used in statistics to visually display and relate two quantitative variables of a multidimensional data set by displaying the data as a collection of points, each having one coordinate on a horizontal and one on a vertical axis.
a. Thing
c. Undefined
b. Scatterplot0
d. Undefined

## Chapter 4. Exponential and Logarithmic Functions

48. _____ is a notation for writing numbers that is often used by scientists and mathematicians to make it easier to write large and small numbers.
    a. Thing
    b. Scientific notation0
    c. Undefined
    d. Undefined

49. A _____ is a statement or claimt that a particular event will occur in the future in more certain terms than a forecast.
    a. Prediction0
    b. Thing
    c. Undefined
    d. Undefined

50. _____ is the transport of people on a trip/journey or the process or time involved in a person or object moving from one location to another.
    a. Travel0
    b. Thing
    c. Undefined
    d. Undefined

51. _____ of an object is its speed in a particular direction.
    a. Thing
    b. Velocity0
    c. Undefined
    d. Undefined

52. _____ is a mathematical science pertaining to the collection, analysis, interpretation or explanation, and presentation of data. It is applicable to a wide variety of academic disciplines, from the physical and social sciences to the humanities.
    a. Statistics0
    b. Thing
    c. Undefined
    d. Undefined

53. In mathematics, an _____, mean, or central tendency of a data set refers to a measure of the "middle" or "expected" value of the data set.
    a. Concept
    b. Average0
    c. Undefined
    d. Undefined

54. _____ is the production of food, feed, fiber, fuel and other goods by the systematic raizing of plants and animals.
    a. Agriculture0
    b. Thing
    c. Undefined
    d. Undefined

55. The metre (or _____, see spelling differences) is a measure of length. It is the basic unit of length in the metric system and in the International System of Units (SI), used around the world for general and scientific purposes.
    a. Concept
    b. Meter0
    c. Undefined
    d. Undefined

56. _____ is a function of the form
    a. Thing
    b. Cubic function0
    c. Undefined
    d. Undefined

57. _____ or investing is a term with several closely-related meanings in business management, finance and economics, related to saving or deferring consumption.

a. Thing  
c. Undefined  
b. Investment0  
d. Undefined  

58. In mathematics and logic, a _____ proof is a way of showing the truth or falsehood of a given statement by a straightforward combination of established facts, usually existing lemmas and theorems, without making any further assumptions.
a. Thing  
c. Undefined  
b. Direct0  
d. Undefined  

59. _____ has many meanings, most of which simply .
a. Thing  
c. Undefined  
b. Power0  
d. Undefined  

60. A _____ is a unit of length, usually used to measure distance, in a number of different systems, including Imperial units, United States customary units and Norwegian/Swedish mil. Its size can vary from system to system, but in each is between 1 and 10 kilometers. In contemporary English contexts _____ refers to either:
a. Thing  
c. Undefined  
b. Mile0  
d. Undefined  

61. _____ is a unit of speed, expressing the number of international miles covered per hour.
a. Miles per hour0  
c. Undefined  
b. Thing  
d. Undefined  

62. _____ is a physical property of a system that underlies the common notions of hot and cold; something that is hotter has the greater _____.
a. Temperature0  
c. Undefined  
b. Thing  
d. Undefined  

63. A _____ is a special kind of ratio, indicating a relationship between two measurements with different units, such as miles to gallons or cents to pounds.
a. Thing  
c. Undefined  
b. Rate0  
d. Undefined  

64. _____ is the fee paid on borrowed money.
a. Interest0  
c. Undefined  
b. Thing  
d. Undefined  

65. An _____ is the fee paid on borrow money.
a. Interest rate0  
c. Undefined  
b. Concept  
d. Undefined  

66. _____ is a free computer algebra system based on a 1982 version of Macsyma
a. Maxima0  
c. Undefined  
b. Thing  
d. Undefined

## Chapter 4. Exponential and Logarithmic Functions

67. _____ are points in the domain of a function at which the function takes a largest value or smallest value, either within a given neighborhood or on the function domain in its entirety.
   a. Maxima and minima0
   b. Thing
   c. Undefined
   d. Undefined

68. In mathematics, maxima and _____, known collectively as extrema, are points in the domain of a function at which the function takes a largest value .
   a. Thing
   b. Minima0
   c. Undefined
   d. Undefined

69. A _____ is a method of using property as security for the payment of a debt.
   a. Thing
   b. Mortgage0
   c. Undefined
   d. Undefined

70. A _____ is a polynomial function of the form $f(x) = ax^2 + bx + c$, where a, b, c are real numbers and a , 0.
   a. Quadratic function0
   b. Event
   c. Undefined
   d. Undefined

71. The _____, the average in everyday English, which is also called the arithmetic _____ (and is distinguished from the geometric _____ or harmonic _____). The average is also called the sample _____. The expected value of a random variable, which is also called the population _____.
   a. Mean0
   b. Thing
   c. Undefined
   d. Undefined

72. In geometry, the _____ of an object is a point in some sense in the middle of the object.
   a. Thing
   b. Center0
   c. Undefined
   d. Undefined

73. In Euclidean geometry, a _____ is the set of all points in a plane at a fixed distance, called the radius, from a given point, the center.
   a. Thing
   b. Circle0
   c. Undefined
   d. Undefined

74. In classical geometry, a _____ of a circle or sphere is any line segment from its center to its boundary. By extension, the _____ of a circle or sphere is the length of any such segment. The _____ is half the diameter. In science and engineering the term _____ of curvature is commonly used as a synonym for _____.
   a. Thing
   b. Radius0
   c. Undefined
   d. Undefined

75. In geometry, a _____ (Greek words diairo = divide and metro = measure) of a circle is any straight line segment that passes through the centre and whose endpoints are on the circular boundary, or, in more modern usage, the length of such a line segment. When using the word in the more modern sense, one speaks of the _____ rather than a _____, because all diameters of a circle have the same length. This length is twice the radius. The _____ of a circle is also the longest chord that the circle has.

a. Thing  
b. Diameter0  
c. Undefined  
d. Undefined  

76. The _____ is a theorem for finding out the factors of a polynomial.
   a. Thing
   b. Factor theorem0
   c. Undefined
   d. Undefined

77. A _____ is the part of the dividend that is left over when the dividend is not evenly divisible by the divisor.
   a. Thing
   b. Remainder0
   c. Undefined
   d. Undefined

78. In mathematics, a _____ is the end result of a division problem. It can also be expressed as the number of times the divisor divides into the dividend.
   a. Thing
   b. Quotient0
   c. Undefined
   d. Undefined

79. _____ is a payment made by a company to its shareholders
   a. Thing
   b. Dividend0
   c. Undefined
   d. Undefined

80. In mathematics, a _____ of an integer n, also called a factor of n, is an integer which evenly divides n without leaving a remainder.
   a. Divisor0
   b. Thing
   c. Undefined
   d. Undefined

81. _____ or arithmetics is the oldest and most elementary branch of mathematics, used by almost everyone, for tasks ranging from simple daily counting to advanced science and business calculations.
   a. Arithmetic0
   b. Thing
   c. Undefined
   d. Undefined

82. _____ in algebra is an application of polynomial long division.
   a. Remainder theorem0
   b. Thing
   c. Undefined
   d. Undefined

83. In mathematics and the mathematical sciences, a _____ is a fixed, but possibly unspecified, value. This is in contrast to a variable, which is not fixed.
   a. Thing
   b. Constant0
   c. Undefined
   d. Undefined

84. A _____ is a symbol or group of symbols, or a word in a natural language that represents a number.
   a. Numeral0
   b. Thing
   c. Undefined
   d. Undefined

85. In mathematics, computing, linguistics, and related disciplines, an _____ is a finite list of well-defined instructions for accomplishing some task which, given an initial state, will terminate in a defined end-state.

## Chapter 4. Exponential and Logarithmic Functions

a. Concept
b. Algorithm0
c. Undefined
d. Undefined

86. In mathematics, _____ allows the rapid division of any polynomial by a binomial of the form x − r. It was described by Paolo Ruffini in 1809. _____ is a special case of long division when the divisor is a linear factor.
a. Thing
b. Ruffini's rule0
c. Undefined
d. Undefined

87. A pair of angles is _____ if their respective measures sum to 180 degrees.
a. Concept
b. Supplementary0
c. Undefined
d. Undefined

88. In mathematics, a _____ is a demonstration that, assuming certain axioms, some statement is necessarily true.
a. Proof0
b. Thing
c. Undefined
d. Undefined

89. In arithmetic, _____ is a procedure for calculating the division of one integer, called the dividend, by another integer called the divisor, to produce a result called the quotient.
a. Long division0
b. Thing
c. Undefined
d. Undefined

90. A _____ is one of the basic shapes of geometry: a polygon with three vertices and three sides which are straight line segments.
a. Thing
b. Triangle0
c. Undefined
d. Undefined

91. A _____ is the result of the addition of a set of numbers. The numbers may be natural numbers, complex numbers, matrices, or still more complicated objects. An infinite _____ is a subtle procedure known as a series.
a. Sum0
b. Thing
c. Undefined
d. Undefined

92. In mathematics, a _____ is a number in the form of a + bi where a and b are real numbers, and i is the imaginary unit, with the property i 2 = −1. The real number a is called the real part of the _____, and the real number b is the imaginary part.
a. Complex number0
b. Thing
c. Undefined
d. Undefined

93. _____ is a branch of mathematics concerning the study of structure, relation and quantity.
a. Algebra0
b. Concept
c. Undefined
d. Undefined

94. In number theory, the _____ of arithmetic (or unique factorization theorem) states that every natural number greater than 1 can be written as a unique product of prime numbers.
a. Fundamental theorem0
b. Concept
c. Undefined
d. Undefined

## Chapter 4. Exponential and Logarithmic Functions

95. _____ states that every non-zero single-variable polynomial, with complex coefficients, has exactly as many complex roots as its degree, if repeated roots are counted up to their multiplicity.
- a. Thing
- b. Fundamental theorem of algebra0
- c. Undefined
- d. Undefined

96. In algebra, a _____ is a binomial formed by taking the opposite of the second term of a binomial.
- a. Conjugate0
- b. Thing
- c. Undefined
- d. Undefined

97. The term _____ can refer to an integer which is the square of some other integer, or an algebraic expression that can be factored as the square of some other expression.
- a. Perfect square0
- b. Thing
- c. Undefined
- d. Undefined

98. The _____ are the only integral domain whose positive elements are well-ordered, and in which order is preserved by addition. Like the natural numbers, the _____ form a countably infinite set. The set of all _____ is usually denoted in mathematics by a boldface Z .
- a. Thing
- b. Integers0
- c. Undefined
- d. Undefined

99. A quadratic equation with real solutions, called roots, which may be real or complex, is given by the _____: $x = \frac{-b \pm \sqrt{b^2 - 4ac}}{2a}$.
- a. Quadratic formula0
- b. Thing
- c. Undefined
- d. Undefined

100. A _____ is a polynomial consisting of three terms; in other words, it is the sum of three monomials.
- a. Trinomial0
- b. Thing
- c. Undefined
- d. Undefined

101. _____ is a fixed, but possibly unspecified, value. This is in contrast to a variable, which is not fixed.
- a. Constant term0
- b. Thing
- c. Undefined
- d. Undefined

102. _____ was a highly influential French philosopher, mathematician, scientist, and writer. Dubbed the "Founder of Modern Philosophy", and the "Father of Modern Mathematics". His theories provided the basis for the calculus of Newton and Leibniz, by applying infinitesimal calculus to the tangent line problem, thus permitting the evolution of that branch of modern mathematics
- a. Person
- b. Descartes0
- c. Undefined
- d. Undefined

103. In mathematics, an _____ number is any real number that is not a rational number- that is, it is a number which cannot be expressed as a fraction m/n, where m and n are integers.
- a. Irrational0
- b. Thing
- c. Undefined
- d. Undefined

## Chapter 4. Exponential and Logarithmic Functions

104. In geometry, a _____ is a special kind of point, usually a corner of a polygon, polyhedron, or higher dimensional polytope. In the geometry of curves a _____ is a point of where the first derivative of curvature is zero. In graph theory, a _____ is the fundamental unit out of which graphs are formed
   a. Vertex0
   b. Thing
   c. Undefined
   d. Undefined

105. _____ means "constancy", i.e. if something retains a certain feature even after we change a way of looking at it, then it is symmetric.
   a. Symmetry0
   b. Thing
   c. Undefined
   d. Undefined

106. An _____ is a straight line around which a geometric figure can be rotated.
   a. Thing
   b. Axis0
   c. Undefined
   d. Undefined

107. _____ of a two-dimensional figure is a line such that, if a perpendicular is constructed, any two points lying on the perpendicular at equal distances from the _____ are identical.
   a. Axis of symmetry0
   b. Thing
   c. Undefined
   d. Undefined

108. The _____ of measurement are a globally standardized and modernized form of the metric system.
   a. Thing
   b. Units0
   c. Undefined
   d. Undefined

109. A _____ is the part of a fraction that tells how many equal parts make up a whole, and which is used in the name of the fraction: "halves", "thirds", "fourths" or "quarters", "fifths" and so on.
   a. Concept
   b. Denominator0
   c. Undefined
   d. Undefined

110. In statistics, _____ means the most frequent value assumed by a random variable, or occurring in a sampling of a random variable.
   a. Mode0
   b. Concept
   c. Undefined
   d. Undefined

111. In geometry, a line _____ is a part of a line that is bounded by two end points, and contains every point on the line between its end points.
   a. Segment0
   b. Concept
   c. Undefined
   d. Undefined

112. A _____ is a part of a line that is bounded by two end points, and contains every point on the line between its end points.
   a. Line segment0
   b. Thing
   c. Undefined
   d. Undefined

113. _____ is a straight line or curve A to which another curve B the one being studied approaches closer and closer as one moves along it.

a. Vertical asymptote0    b. Thing
c. Undefined              d. Undefined

114. An _____ is a straight line or curve A to which another curve B approaches closer and closer as one moves along it. As one moves along B, the space between it and the _____ A becomes smaller and smaller, and can in fact be made as small as one could wish by going far enough along. A curve may or may not touch or cross its _____. In fact, the curve may intersect the _____ an infinite number of times.
a. Asymptote0             b. Thing
c. Undefined              d. Undefined

115. _____ is the largest positive integer that divides both numbers without remainder.
a. Common Factor0         b. Thing
c. Undefined              d. Undefined

116. In astronomy, geography, geometry and related sciences and contexts, a plane is said to be _____ at a given point if it is locally perpendicular to the gradient of the gravity field, i.e., with the direction of the gravitational force at that point.
a. Thing                  b. Horizontal0
c. Undefined              d. Undefined

117. _____ are objects, characters, or other concrete representations of ideas, concepts, or other abstractions.
a. Thing                  b. Symbols0
c. Undefined              d. Undefined

118. A _____ is a numeral used to indicate a count. The most common use of the word today is to name the part of a fraction that tells the number or count of equal parts.
a. Numerator0             b. Thing
c. Undefined              d. Undefined

119. A _____ is a quantity that denotes the proportional amount or magnitude of one quantity relative to another.
a. Ratio0                 b. Thing
c. Undefined              d. Undefined

120. An _____ is a combination of numbers, operators, grouping symbols and/or free variables and bound variables arranged in a meaningful way which can be evaluated..
a. Expression0            b. Thing
c. Undefined              d. Undefined

121. _____ is a mathematical subject that includes the study of limits, derivatives, integrals, and power series and constitutes a major part of modern university curriculum.
a. Calculus0              b. Thing
c. Undefined              d. Undefined

122. In mathematics, an inequality is a statement about the relative size or order of two objects. For example 14 > 10, or 14 is _____ 10.

## Chapter 4. Exponential and Logarithmic Functions

a. Thing
c. Undefined
b. Greater than0
d. Undefined

123. In geometry, an _____ angle is an angle that is not a 90 degree angle, or an angle that is divisible by 90: 180, 270, 360/0
a. Thing
c. Undefined
b. Oblique0
d. Undefined

124. Equivalence is the condition of being _____ or essentially equal.
a. Equivalent0
c. Undefined
b. Thing
d. Undefined

125. In mathematics, the conjugate _____ or adjoint matrix of an m-by-n matrix A with complex entries is the n-by-m matrix A* obtained from A by taking the transpose and then taking the complex conjugate of each entry.
a. Pairs0
c. Undefined
b. Thing
d. Undefined

126. _____ is a temperature scale named after the German physicist Daniel Gabriel _____ , who proposed it in 1724.
a. Thing
c. Undefined
b. Fahrenheit0
d. Undefined

127. _____, in economics and political economy, are the distributions or payments awarded to the various suppliers of the factors of production.
a. Returns0
c. Undefined
b. Thing
d. Undefined

128. In sociology and biology a _____ is the collection of people or organisms of a particular species living in a given geographic area or space, usually measured by a census.
a. Population0
c. Undefined
b. Thing
d. Undefined

129. _____ is often used to describe the measurement of the steepness, incline, gradient, or grade of a straight line. The _____ is defined as the ratio of the "rise" divided by the "run" between two points on a line, or in other words, the ratio of the altitude change to the horizontal distance between any two points on the line.
a. Slope0
c. Undefined
b. Thing
d. Undefined

130. _____ are functions which satisfy particular symmetry relations, with respect to taking additive inverses.
a. Thing
c. Undefined
b. Even function0
d. Undefined

131. Any point where a graph makes contact with an coordinate axis is called an _____ of the graph
a. Thing
c. Undefined
b. Intercept0
d. Undefined

## Chapter 4. Exponential and Logarithmic Functions

132. The function difference divided by the point difference is known as the _____
    a. Difference quotient0
    b. Thing
    c. Undefined
    d. Undefined

133. _____ is the middle point of a line segment.
    a. Midpoint0
    b. Thing
    c. Undefined
    d. Undefined

134. _____ systems represent systems whose behavior is not expressible as a sum of the behaviors of its descriptors.
    a. Thing
    b. Nonlinear0
    c. Undefined
    d. Undefined

135. In combinatorial mathematics, a _____ is an un-ordered collection of unique elements.
    a. Combination0
    b. Concept
    c. Undefined
    d. Undefined

136. In mathematics, an _____ is a statement about the relative size or order of two objects.
    a. Thing
    b. Inequality0
    c. Undefined
    d. Undefined

137. A _____ is a set of possible values that a variable can take on in order to satisfy a given set of conditions, which may include equations and inequalities.
    a. Solution set0
    b. Thing
    c. Undefined
    d. Undefined

138. _____ is the notation in which permitted values for a variable are expressed as ranging over a certain interval; "5 < x < 9" is an example of the application of _____.
    a. Thing
    b. Interval notation0
    c. Undefined
    d. Undefined

139. In geometry, an _____ is a point at which a line segment or ray terminates.
    a. Endpoint0
    b. Thing
    c. Undefined
    d. Undefined

140. A _____ is a symbolic representation denoting a quantity or expression. It often represents an "unknown" quantity that has the potential to change.
    a. Thing
    b. Variable0
    c. Undefined
    d. Undefined

141. _____, from Latin meaning "to make progress", is defined in two different ways. Pure economic _____ is the increase in wealth that an investor has from making an investment, taking into consideration all costs associated with that investment including the opportunity cost of capital.
    a. Thing
    b. Profit0
    c. Undefined
    d. Undefined

## Chapter 4. Exponential and Logarithmic Functions

142. The _____ integers are all the integers from zero on upwards.
   a. Thing
   b. Nonnegative0
   c. Undefined
   d. Undefined

143. In geometry a _____ is a plane figure that is bounded by a closed path or circuit, composed of a finite number of sequential line segments.
   a. Polygon0
   b. Thing
   c. Undefined
   d. Undefined

144. A _____ can refer to a line joining two nonadjacent vertices of a polygon or polyhedron, or in some contexts any upward or downward sloping line. .
   a. Diagonal0
   b. Thing
   c. Undefined
   d. Undefined

145. _____ element of an element x with respect to a binary operation * with identity element e is an element y such that x * y = y * x = e. In particular,
   a. Thing
   b. Inverse0
   c. Undefined
   d. Undefined

146. _____ is the relationship between two variables, like a ratio in which the two quantities being compared are different units.
   a. Thing
   b. Direct variation0
   c. Undefined
   d. Undefined

147. _____ is a kind of property which exists as magnitude or multitude. It is among the basic classes of things along with quality, substance, change, and relation.
   a. Amount0
   b. Thing
   c. Undefined
   d. Undefined

148. In mathematics, two quantities are called _____ if they vary in such a way that one of the quantities is a constant multiple of the other, or equivalently if they have a constant ratio.
   a. Thing
   b. Proportional0
   c. Undefined
   d. Undefined

149. _____ is a special mathematical relationship between two quantities.Two quantities are called proportional if they vary in such a way that one of the quantities is a constant multiple of the other, or equivalently if they have a constant ratio.
   a. Proportionality0
   b. Thing
   c. Undefined
   d. Undefined

150. An _____ is a term used to describe an allocation of money from one person to another.
   a. Thing
   b. Allowance0
   c. Undefined
   d. Undefined

151. In mathematics and more specifically set theory, the _____ set is the unique set which contains no elements.

## Chapter 4. Exponential and Logarithmic Functions

a. Empty0  
b. Thing  
c. Undefined  
d. Undefined

152. In mathematics, _____ geometry was the traditional name for the geometry of three-dimensional Euclidean space — for practical purposes the kind of space we live in.
a. Thing  
b. Solid0  
c. Undefined  
d. Undefined

153. In physics, _____ is an influence that may cause an object to accelerate. It may be experienced as a lift, a push, or a pull. The actual acceleration of the body is determined by the vector sum of all forces acting on it, known as net _____ or resultant _____.
a. Force0  
b. Thing  
c. Undefined  
d. Undefined

154. _____ is electromagnetic radiation with a wavelength that is visible to the eye (visible _____) or, in a technical or scientific context, electromagnetic radiation of any wavelength.
a. Thing  
b. Light0  
c. Undefined  
d. Undefined

155. In mathematics, the _____ of a coordinate system is the point where the axes of the system intersect.
a. Origin0  
b. Thing  
c. Undefined  
d. Undefined

156. The _____ of a solid object is the three-dimensional concept of how much space it occupies, often quantified numerically.
a. Thing  
b. Volume0  
c. Undefined  
d. Undefined

157. In mathematics, a _____ is a quadric surface, with the following equation in Cartesian coordinates: $(x/_a)^2 + (y/_b)^2 = 1$.
a. Cylinder0  
b. Thing  
c. Undefined  
d. Undefined

158. A _____ is a three-dimensional solid object bounded by six square faces, facets, or sides, with three meeting at each vertex.
a. Thing  
b. Cube0  
c. Undefined  
d. Undefined

159. A _____ is a vehicle, missile or aircraft which obtains thrust by the reaction to the ejection of fast moving fluid from within a _____ engine.
a. Thing  
b. Rocket0  
c. Undefined  
d. Undefined

160. The _____, in practice often shortened to amp, is a unit of electric current, or amount of electric charge per second.

a. Amperes0  b. Thing
c. Undefined  d. Undefined

## Chapter 5. Systems of Equations and Matrices

1. The mathematical concept of a _____ expresses the intuitive idea of deterministic dependence between two quantities, one of which is viewed as primary and the other as secondary. A _____ then is a way to associate a unique output for each input of a specified type, for example, a real number or an element of a given set.
   a. Function0
   b. Thing
   c. Undefined
   d. Undefined

2. A _____ is a set of numbers that designate location in a given reference system, such as x,y in a planar _____ system or an x,y,z in a three-dimensional _____ system.
   a. Thing
   b. Coordinate0
   c. Undefined
   d. Undefined

3. _____ element of an element x with respect to a binary operation * with identity element e is an element y such that x * y = y * x = e. In particular,
   a. Thing
   b. Inverse0
   c. Undefined
   d. Undefined

4. An _____ is a collection of two not necessarily distinct objects, one of which is distinguished as the first coordinate and the other as the second coordinate.
   a. Ordered pair0
   b. Thing
   c. Undefined
   d. Undefined

5. In mathematics, a _____ (also spelled reflexion) is a map that transforms an object into its mirror image.
   a. Reflection0
   b. Concept
   c. Undefined
   d. Undefined

6. In mathematics, the conjugate _____ or adjoint matrix of an m-by-n matrix A with complex entries is the n-by-m matrix A* obtained from A by taking the transpose and then taking the complex conjugate of each entry.
   a. Pairs0
   b. Thing
   c. Undefined
   d. Undefined

7. In mathematics, the _____ of a function is the set of all "output" values produced by that function. Given a function $f : A \to B$, the _____ of $f$, is defined to be the set $\{x \in B : x = f(a) \text{ for some } a \in A\}$.
   a. Range0
   b. Thing
   c. Undefined
   d. Undefined

8. In mathematics, a _____ of a k-place relation $L \subseteq X_1 \times \ldots \times X_k$ is one of the sets $X_j$, $1 \le j \le k$. In the special case where k = 2 and $L \subseteq X_1 \times X_2$ is a function $L : X_1 \to X_2$, it is conventional to refer to $X_1$ as the _____ of the function and to refer to $X_2$ as the codomain of the function.
   a. Domain0
   b. Thing
   c. Undefined
   d. Undefined

9. Acid _____ ratio measures the ability of a company to use its near cash or quick assets to immediately extinguish its current liabilities.
   a. Test0
   b. Thing
   c. Undefined
   d. Undefined

10. Equivalence is the condition of being _____ or essentially equal.

## Chapter 5. Systems of Equations and Matrices    69

a. Thing  
c. Undefined  
b. Equivalent0  
d. Undefined

11. In astronomy, geography, geometry and related sciences and contexts, a plane is said to be _____ at a given point if it is locally perpendicular to the gradient of the gravity field, i.e., with the direction of the gravitational force at that point.
a. Horizontal0  
c. Undefined  
b. Thing  
d. Undefined

12. In mathematics, the _____ f is the collection of all ordered pairs . In particular, graph means the graphical representation of this collection, in the form of a curve or surface, together with axes, etc. Graphing on a Cartesian plane is sometimes referred to as curve sketching.
a. Thing  
c. Undefined  
b. Graph of a function0  
d. Undefined

13. In mathematics, _____ growth occurs when the growth rate of a function is always proportional to the function's current size.
a. Exponential0  
c. Undefined  
b. Thing  
d. Undefined

14. _____ are the basic objects of study in graph theory. Informally speaking, a graph is a set of objects called points, nodes, or vertices connected by links called lines or edges.
a. Graphs0  
c. Undefined  
b. Thing  
d. Undefined

15. An _____ is a function which does the reverse of a given function.
a. Inverse function0  
c. Undefined  
b. Thing  
d. Undefined

16. In geographic information systems, a _____ comprises an entity with a geographic location, typically determined by points, arcs, or polygons. Carriageways and cadastres exemplify _____ data.
a. Thing  
c. Undefined  
b. Feature0  
d. Undefined

17. In mathematics, a _____ of a positive integer n is a way of writing n as a sum of positive integers.
a. Thing  
c. Undefined  
b. Composition0  
d. Undefined

18. An _____ is when two lines intersect somewhere on a plane creating a right angle at intersection
a. Thing  
c. Undefined  
b. Axes0  
d. Undefined

19. _____ is the transport of people on a trip/journey or the process or time involved in a person or object moving from one location to another.
a. Thing  
c. Undefined  
b. Travel0  
d. Undefined

## Chapter 5. Systems of Equations and Matrices

20. A _____ is a unit of length, usually used to measure distance, in a number of different systems, including Imperial units, United States customary units and Norwegian/Swedish mil. Its size can vary from system to system, but in each is between 1 and 10 kilometers. In contemporary English contexts _____ refers to either:
   a. Thing
   b. Mile0
   c. Undefined
   d. Undefined

21. _____ is a unit of speed, expressing the number of international miles covered per hour.
   a. Miles per hour0
   b. Thing
   c. Undefined
   d. Undefined

22. The word _____ comes from the Latin word linearis, which means created by lines.
   a. Linear0
   b. Thing
   c. Undefined
   d. Undefined

23. A _____ is a first degree polynomial mathematical function of the form: f(x) = mx + b where m and b are real constants and x is a real variable.
   a. Linear function0
   b. Thing
   c. Undefined
   d. Undefined

24. _____ is the production of food, feed, fiber, fuel and other goods by the systematic raizing of plants and animals.
   a. Agriculture0
   b. Thing
   c. Undefined
   d. Undefined

25. _____ is one of the most important functions in mathematics. A function commonly used to study growth and decay
   a. Exponential function0
   b. Thing
   c. Undefined
   d. Undefined

26. A _____ is 360° or 2δ radians.
   a. Turn0
   b. Thing
   c. Undefined
   d. Undefined

27. In mathematics, a _____ may be described informally as a number that can be given by an infinite decimal representation.
   a. Real number0
   b. Thing
   c. Undefined
   d. Undefined

28. In mathematics and the mathematical sciences, a _____ is a fixed, but possibly unspecified, value. This is in contrast to a variable, which is not fixed.
   a. Constant0
   b. Thing
   c. Undefined
   d. Undefined

29. _____ is a function whose values do not vary and thus are constant.
   a. Constant function0
   b. Thing
   c. Undefined
   d. Undefined

## Chapter 5. Systems of Equations and Matrices

30. In mathematics, the concept of a _____ tries to capture the intuitive idea of a geometrical one-dimensional and continuous object. A simple example is the circle.
    a. Curve0
    b. Thing
    c. Undefined
    d. Undefined

31. An _____ is a straight line or curve A to which another curve B approaches closer and closer as one moves along it. As one moves along B, the space between it and the _____ A becomes smaller and smaller, and can in fact be made as small as one could wish by going far enough along. A curve may or may not touch or cross its _____. In fact, the curve may intersect the _____ an infinite number of times.
    a. Thing
    b. Asymptote0
    c. Undefined
    d. Undefined

32. In Euclidean geometry, a _____ is moving every point a constant distance in a specified direction.
    a. Translation0
    b. Concept
    c. Undefined
    d. Undefined

33. The _____ of a ring $R$ is defined to be the smallest positive integer $n$ such that $n\,a = 0$, for all a in R.
    a. Thing
    b. Characteristic0
    c. Undefined
    d. Undefined

34. The _____ of measurement are a globally standardized and modernized form of the metric system.
    a. Units0
    b. Thing
    c. Undefined
    d. Undefined

35. A _____ is a special kind of ratio, indicating a relationship between two measurements with different units, such as miles to gallons or cents to pounds.
    a. Rate0
    b. Thing
    c. Undefined
    d. Undefined

36. _____ is a kind of property which exists as magnitude or multitude. It is among the basic classes of things along with quality, substance, change, and relation.
    a. Thing
    b. Amount0
    c. Undefined
    d. Undefined

37. _____ is the fee paid on borrowed money.
    a. Thing
    b. Interest0
    c. Undefined
    d. Undefined

38. An _____ is the fee paid on borrow money.
    a. Concept
    b. Interest rate0
    c. Undefined
    d. Undefined

39. In business, particularly accounting, a _____ is the time intervals that the accounts, statement, payments, or other calculations cover.

## Chapter 5. Systems of Equations and Matrices

a. Period0  
b. Thing  
c. Undefined  
d. Undefined  

40. Leonhard _____ was a pioneering Swiss mathematician and physicist, who spent most of his life in Russia and Germany.
    a. Person  
    b. Euler0  
    c. Undefined  
    d. Undefined  

41. In mathematics, an _____ number is any real number that is not a rational number- that is, it is a number which cannot be expressed as a fraction m/n, where m and n are integers.
    a. Thing  
    b. Irrational0  
    c. Undefined  
    d. Undefined  

42. _____ interest refers to the fact that whenever interest is calculated, it is based not only on the original principal, but also on any unpaid interest that has been added to the principal.
    a. Thing  
    b. Compound0  
    c. Undefined  
    d. Undefined  

43. _____ refers to the fact that whenever interest is calculated, it is based not only on the original principal, but also on any unpaid interest that has been added to the principal. The more frequently interest is compounded, the faster the balance grows.
    a. Concept  
    b. Compound interest0  
    c. Undefined  
    d. Undefined  

44. In banking and accountancy, the outstanding _____ is the amount of money owned, or due, that remains in a deposit account or a loan account at a given date, after all past remittances, payments and withdrawal have been accounted for.
    a. Balance0  
    b. Thing  
    c. Undefined  
    d. Undefined  

45. _____ usually refers to money in the form of liquid currency, such as banknotes or coins.
    a. Cash0  
    b. Thing  
    c. Undefined  
    d. Undefined  

46. In common philosophical language, a proposition or _____, is the content of an assertion, that is, it is true-or-false and defined by the meaning of a particular piece of language.
    a. Statement0  
    b. Concept  
    c. Undefined  
    d. Undefined  

47. In economics, supply and _____ describe market relations between prospective sellers and buyers of a good.
    a. Thing  
    b. Demand0  
    c. Undefined  
    d. Undefined  

48. _____ has many meanings, most of which simply .

## Chapter 5. Systems of Equations and Matrices

a. Power0  
b. Thing  
c. Undefined  
d. Undefined

49. In mathematics, a _____ of a number x is the exponent y of the power by such that $x = b^y$. The value used for the base b must be neither 0 nor 1, nor a root of 1 in the case of the extension to complex numbers, and is typically 10, e, or 2.
    a. Logarithm0  
    b. Thing  
    c. Undefined  
    d. Undefined

50. The _____, the average in everyday English, which is also called the arithmetic _____ (and is distinguished from the geometric _____ or harmonic _____). The average is also called the sample _____. The expected value of a random variable, which is also called the population _____.
    a. Mean0  
    b. Thing  
    c. Undefined  
    d. Undefined

51. In mathematics, an inequality is a statement about the relative size or order of two objects. For example 14 > 10, or 14 is _____ 10.
    a. Greater than0  
    b. Thing  
    c. Undefined  
    d. Undefined

52. A _____ function is a function for which, intuitively, small changes in the input result in small changes in the output.
    a. Continuous0  
    b. Event  
    c. Undefined  
    d. Undefined

53. _____ is a straight line or curve A to which another curve B the one being studied approaches closer and closer as one moves along it.
    a. Thing  
    b. Vertical asymptote0  
    c. Undefined  
    d. Undefined

54. In mathematics, the _____ is the logarithm with base 10.
    a. Thing  
    b. Common logarithm0  
    c. Undefined  
    d. Undefined

55. In statistics, _____ means the most frequent value assumed by a random variable, or occurring in a sampling of a random variable.
    a. Mode0  
    b. Concept  
    c. Undefined  
    d. Undefined

56. A _____ is a negotiable instrument instructing a financial institution to pay a specific amount of a specific currency from a specific demand account held in the maker/depositor's name with that institution. Both the maker and payee may be natural persons or legal entities.
    a. Check0  
    b. Thing  
    c. Undefined  
    d. Undefined

57. A _____ is a number that is less than zero.

## Chapter 5. Systems of Equations and Matrices

a. Thing
c. Undefined
b. Negative number0
d. Undefined

58. _____ is the logarithm to the base e, where e is an irrational constant approximately equal to 2.718281828459.
a. Thing
c. Undefined
b. Natural logarithm0
d. Undefined

59. In mathematics, an _____, mean, or central tendency of a data set refers to a measure of the "middle" or "expected" value of the data set.
a. Concept
c. Undefined
b. Average0
d. Undefined

60. In sociology and biology a _____ is the collection of people or organisms of a particular species living in a given geographic area or space, usually measured by a census.
a. Population0
c. Undefined
b. Thing
d. Undefined

61. In mathematics, _____ expressions is used to reduce the expression into the lowest possible term.
a. Simplifying0
c. Undefined
b. Thing
d. Undefined

62. The _____ of a mathematical object is its size: a property by which it can be larger or smaller than other objects of the same kind; in technical terms, an ordering of the class of objects to which it belongs.
a. Thing
c. Undefined
b. Magnitude0
d. Undefined

63. In Euclidean geometry, a uniform _____ is a linear transformation that enlargers or diminishes objects, and whose _____ factor is the same in all directions. This is also called homothethy.
a. Thing
c. Undefined
b. Scale0
d. Undefined

64. An _____ is the result from the sudden release of stored energy in the Earth's crust that creates seismic waves.
a. Thing
c. Undefined
b. Earthquake0
d. Undefined

65. In elementary algebra, an _____ is a set that contains every real number between two indicated numbers and may contain the two numbers themselves.
a. Thing
c. Undefined
b. Interval0
d. Undefined

66. Mathematical _____ is used to represent ideas.
a. Notation0
c. Undefined
b. Thing
d. Undefined

67. _____ is a notation for writing numbers that is often used by scientists and mathematicians to make it easier to write large and small numbers.

## Chapter 5. Systems of Equations and Matrices

a. Scientific notation0  
b. Thing  
c. Undefined  
d. Undefined

68. The _____ relative to a specified or implied reference level.
a. Decibel0  
b. Thing  
c. Undefined  
d. Undefined

69. In mathematics, _____ allows the rapid division of any polynomial by a binomial of the form x − r. It was described by Paolo Ruffini in 1809. _____ is a special case of long division when the divisor is a linear factor.
a. Ruffini's rule0  
b. Thing  
c. Undefined  
d. Undefined

70. In mathematics, there are several meanings of _____ depending on the subject.
a. Thing  
b. Degree0  
c. Undefined  
d. Undefined

71. In mathematics, a _____ is an expression that is constructed from one or more variables and constants, using only the operations of addition, subtraction, multiplication, and constant positive whole number exponents. is a _____. Note in particular that division by an expression containing a variable is not in general allowed in polynomials. [1]
a. Thing  
b. Polynomial0  
c. Undefined  
d. Undefined

72. Any point where a graph makes contact with an coordinate axis is called an _____ of the graph
a. Intercept0  
b. Thing  
c. Undefined  
d. Undefined

73. In mathematics, a _____ is the result of multiplying, or an expression that identifies factors to be multiplied.
a. Product0  
b. Thing  
c. Undefined  
d. Undefined

74. The _____ governs the differentiation of products of differentiable functions.
a. Product rule0  
b. Thing  
c. Undefined  
d. Undefined

75. In mathematics, a _____ is a demonstration that, assuming certain axioms, some statement is necessarily true.
a. Thing  
b. Proof0  
c. Undefined  
d. Undefined

76. In mathematics, a _____ is the end result of a division problem. It can also be expressed as the number of times the divisor divides into the dividend.
a. Quotient0  
b. Thing  
c. Undefined  
d. Undefined

77. The _____ is a method of finding the derivative of a function that is the quotient of two other functions for which derivatives exist.

## Chapter 5. Systems of Equations and Matrices

    a. Quotient rule0                                    b. Thing
    c. Undefined                                       d. Undefined

78. _____ is a method for differentiating expressions involving exponentiation the power operation.
    a. Power rule0                                    b. Thing
    c. Undefined                                       d. Undefined

79. A _____ is the result of the addition of a set of numbers. The numbers may be natural numbers, complex numbers, matrices, or still more complicated objects. An infinite _____ is a subtle procedure known as a series.
    a. Thing                                           b. Sum0
    c. Undefined                                       d. Undefined

80. _____ is a concept in traditional logic referring to a "type of immediate inference in which from a given proposition another proposition is inferred which has as its subject the predicate of the original proposition and as its predicate the subject of the original proposition (the quality of the proposition being retained)."
    a. Conversion0                                 b. Concept
    c. Undefined                                       d. Undefined

81. In mathematics and elsewhere, the adjective _____ means fourth order, such as the function x4. A _____ number is a number which equals the fourth power of an integer.
    a. Quartic0                                       b. Thing
    c. Undefined                                       d. Undefined

82. In mathematics, a _____ number is a number which can be expressed as a ratio of two integers. Non-integer _____ numbers (commonly called fractions) are usually written as the vulgar fraction a / b, where b is not zero.
    a. Rational0                                     b. Thing
    c. Undefined                                       d. Undefined

83. A _____ is a symbolic representation denoting a quantity or expression. It often represents an "unknown" quantity that has the potential to change.
    a. Thing                                           b. Variable0
    c. Undefined                                       d. Undefined

84. _____ is a mathematical operation, written $a^n$, involving two numbers, the base a and the exponent n.
    a. Exponentiating0                          b. Thing
    c. Undefined                                       d. Undefined

85. _____ is a mathematical operation, written $a^n$, involving two numbers, the base a and the exponent n.
    a. Thing                                           b. Exponentiation0
    c. Undefined                                       d. Undefined

86. In mathematics, the _____ of two sets A and B is the set that contains all elements of A that also belong to B (or equivalently, all elements of B that also belong to A), but no other elements.
    a. Intersection0                               b. Thing
    c. Undefined                                       d. Undefined

## Chapter 5. Systems of Equations and Matrices

87. Two mathematical objects are equal if and only if they are precisely the same in every way. This defines a binary relation, _____, denoted by the sign of _____ "=" in such a way that the statement "x = y" means that x and y are equal.
    a. Equality0
    b. Thing
    c. Undefined
    d. Undefined

88. A _____ is a deliberate process for transforming one or more inputs into one or more results.
    a. Calculation0
    b. Thing
    c. Undefined
    d. Undefined

89. A quadratic equation with real solutions, called roots, which may be real or complex, is given by the _____: $x = \frac{-b \pm \sqrt{b^2 - 4ac}}{2a}$.
    a. Quadratic formula0
    b. Thing
    c. Undefined
    d. Undefined

90. An _____ is a combination of numbers, operators, grouping symbols and/or free variables and bound variables arranged in a meaningful way which can be evaluated..
    a. Thing
    b. Expression0
    c. Undefined
    d. Undefined

91. In mathematics, _____ is the decomposition of an object into a product of other objects, or factors, which when multiplied together give the original.
    a. Factoring0
    b. Thing
    c. Undefined
    d. Undefined

92. In geometry, a _____ is a special kind of point, usually a corner of a polygon, polyhedron, or higher dimensional polytope. In the geometry of curves a _____ is a point of where the first derivative of curvature is zero. In graph theory, a _____ is the fundamental unit out of which graphs are formed
    a. Thing
    b. Vertex0
    c. Undefined
    d. Undefined

93. _____ is change in population over time, and can be quantified as the change in the number of individuals in a population per unit time.
    a. Population growth0
    b. Thing
    c. Undefined
    d. Undefined

94. In mathematics, _____ occurs when the growth rate of a function is always proportional to the function's current size.
    a. Exponential growth0
    b. Thing
    c. Undefined
    d. Undefined

95. The _____ is the period of time required for a quantity to double in size or value.
    a. Doubling time0
    b. Thing
    c. Undefined
    d. Undefined

## Chapter 5. Systems of Equations and Matrices

96. _____ or investing is a term with several closely-related meanings in business management, finance and economics, related to saving or deferring consumption.
   a. Investment0
   b. Thing
   c. Undefined
   d. Undefined

97. The population _____ is the total number of human beings alive on the planet Earth at a given time.
   a. Of the world0
   b. Thing
   c. Undefined
   d. Undefined

98. The _____ is the total number of human beings alive on the planet Earth at a given time.
   a. World population0
   b. Thing
   c. Undefined
   d. Undefined

99. A _____ models the S-curve of growth of some set P. The initial stage of growth is approximately exponential; then, as saturation begins, the growth slows, and at maturity, growth stops.
   a. Logistic function0
   b. Thing
   c. Undefined
   d. Undefined

100. _____ Any process by which a specified characteristic usually amplitude of the output of a device is prevented from exceeding a predetermined value.
   a. Thing
   b. Limiting0
   c. Undefined
   d. Undefined

101. _____ is a way of expressing a number as a fraction of 100 per cent meaning "per hundred".
   a. Thing
   b. Percent0
   c. Undefined
   d. Undefined

102. A _____ is a type of particle detector that measures ionizing radiation.
   a. Geiger counter0
   b. Thing
   c. Undefined
   d. Undefined

103. A _____ is a function that assigns a number to subsets of a given set.
   a. Measure0
   b. Thing
   c. Undefined
   d. Undefined

104. The _____ integers are all the integers from zero on upwards.
   a. Thing
   b. Nonnegative0
   c. Undefined
   d. Undefined

105. _____ is the process in which an unstable atomic nucleus loses energy by emitting radiation in the form of particles or electromagnetic waves.
   a. Thing
   b. Radioactive decay0
   c. Undefined
   d. Undefined

106. An _____ or member of a set is an object that when collected together make up the set.

## Chapter 5. Systems of Equations and Matrices

a. Thing  
b. Element0  
c. Undefined  
d. Undefined

107. Initial objects are also called _____, and terminal objects are also called final.  
a. Thing  
b. Coterminal0  
c. Undefined  
d. Undefined

108. _____ is a synonym for information.  
a. Data0  
b. Thing  
c. Undefined  
d. Undefined

109. In probability theory and statistics, _____, also called _____ coefficient, indicates the strength and direction of a linear relationship between two random variables.  
a. Thing  
b. Correlation0  
c. Undefined  
d. Undefined

110. In mathematics, a _____ is a constant multiplicative factor of a certain object. The object can be such things as a variable, a vector, a function, etc. For example, the _____ of $9x^2$ is 9.  
a. Thing  
b. Coefficient0  
c. Undefined  
d. Undefined

111. In plane geometry, a _____ is a polygon with four equal sides, four right angles, and parallel opposite sides. In algebra, the _____ of a number is that number multiplied by itself.  
a. Thing  
b. Square0  
c. Undefined  
d. Undefined

112. _____ is a radiometric dating method that uses the naturally occurring isotope carbon-14 to determine the age of carbonaceous materials up to about 60,000 years.  
a. Thing  
b. Radiocarbon dating0  
c. Undefined  
d. Undefined

113. An n-sided _____ is a polyhedron formed by connecting an n-sided polygonal base and a point, called the apex, by n triangular faces. In other words, it is a conic solid with polygonal base.  
a. Pyramid0  
b. Thing  
c. Undefined  
d. Undefined

114. In epidemiology, an _____ is a disease that appears as new cases in a given human population, during a given period, at a rate that substantially exceeds with is "expected," based on recent experience.  
a. Epidemic0  
b. Thing  
c. Undefined  
d. Undefined

115. _____ the expected value of a random variable displays the average or central value of the variable. It is a summary value of the distribution of the variable.  
a. Determining0  
b. Thing  
c. Undefined  
d. Undefined

## Chapter 5. Systems of Equations and Matrices

116. _____ is a physical property of a system that underlies the common notions of hot and cold; something that is hotter has the greater _____.
a. Temperature0
b. Thing
c. Undefined
d. Undefined

117. _____ is a statistical measure of the average length of survival of a living thing.
a. Life expectancy0
b. Thing
c. Undefined
d. Undefined

118. In mathematics, _____ geometry was the traditional name for the geometry of three-dimensional Euclidean space — for practical purposes the kind of space we live in.
a. Solid0
b. Thing
c. Undefined
d. Undefined

119. A _____ is a statement or claimt that a particular event will occur in the future in more certain terms than a forecast.
a. Thing
b. Prediction0
c. Undefined
d. Undefined

120. A _____ signifies a point or points of probability on a subject e.g., the _____ of creativity, which allows for the formation of rule or norm or law by interpretation of the phenomena events that can be created.
a. Thing
b. Principle0
c. Undefined
d. Undefined

121. In mathematics, _____ is an elementary arithmetic operation. When one of the numbers is a whole number, _____ is the repeated sum of the other number.
a. Thing
b. Multiplication0
c. Undefined
d. Undefined

122. In mathematics, a _____ of a number x is a number r such that $r^2 = x$, or in words, a number r whose square (the result of multiplying the number by itself) is x.
a. Square root0
b. Thing
c. Undefined
d. Undefined

123. In mathematics, an _____ is a statement about the relative size or order of two objects.
a. Thing
b. Inequality0
c. Undefined
d. Undefined

124. In mathematics, a _____ of a complex-valued function f is a member x of the domain of f such that f(x) vanishes at x, that is, x : f (x) = 0.
a. Thing
b. Root0
c. Undefined
d. Undefined

125. _____ of a single or multiple future payments is the nominal amounts of money to change hands at some future date, discounted to account for the time value of money, and other factors such as investment risk.

## Chapter 5. Systems of Equations and Matrices

a. Present value0
b. Thing
c. Undefined
d. Undefined

126. In economics, _____ describe market relations between prospective sellers and buyers of a good.
a. Thing
b. Supply and demand0
c. Undefined
d. Undefined

127. In economics, economic _____ is simply a state of the world where economic forces are balanced and in the absence of external influences the values of economic variables will not change.
a. Equilibrium0
b. Thing
c. Undefined
d. Undefined

128. _____ is the price at which the quantity demanded of a good or service is equal to the quantity supplied.
a. Equilibrium price0
b. Thing
c. Undefined
d. Undefined

129. _____ is electromagnetic radiation with a wavelength that is visible to the eye (visible _____ ) or, in a technical or scientific context, electromagnetic radiation of any wavelength.
a. Thing
b. Light0
c. Undefined
d. Undefined

130. A _____ is an individual or household that purchases and uses goods and services generated within the economy.
a. Thing
b. Consumer0
c. Undefined
d. Undefined

131. The payment of _____ as remuneration for services rendered or products sold is a common way to reward sales people.
a. Commission0
b. Thing
c. Undefined
d. Undefined

132. A _____, scatter diagram or scatter graph is a graph used in statistics to visually display and relate two quantitative variables of a multidimensional data set by displaying the data as a collection of points, each having one coordinate on a horizontal and one on a vertical axis.
a. Scatterplot0
b. Thing
c. Undefined
d. Undefined

133. The _____ is the highest point in a certain portion of a graph.
a. Thing
b. Relative maximum0
c. Undefined
d. Undefined

134. A _____ is a set of possible values that a variable can take on in order to satisfy a given set of conditions, which may include equations and inequalities.
a. Solution set0
b. Thing
c. Undefined
d. Undefined

## Chapter 5. Systems of Equations and Matrices

135. _____ are a set of equations containing multiple variables.
  a. Systems of equations0
  b. Thing
  c. Undefined
  d. Undefined

136. A _____ is an equation in which each term is either a constant or the product of a constant times the first power of a variable.
  a. Linear equation0
  b. Thing
  c. Undefined
  d. Undefined

137. _____ is the state of being greater than any finite real or natural number, however large.
  a. Infinite0
  b. Thing
  c. Undefined
  d. Undefined

138. The _____ is used to discard one of the variables in an equation, only to replace it with the actual value when solving multiple equations.
  a. Thing
  b. Substitution method0
  c. Undefined
  d. Undefined

139. The _____ are the only integral domain whose positive elements are well-ordered, and in which order is preserved by addition. Like the natural numbers, the _____ form a countably infinite set. The set of all _____ is usually denoted in mathematics by a boldface Z.
  a. Integers0
  b. Thing
  c. Undefined
  d. Undefined

140. _____, either of the curved-bracket punctuation marks that together make a set of _____
  a. Parentheses0
  b. Thing
  c. Undefined
  d. Undefined

141. The Gaussian _____ is an algorithm which can be used to determine the solutions of a system of linear equations, to find the rank of a matrix, and to calculate the inverse of an invertible square matrix.
  a. Elimination method0
  b. Thing
  c. Undefined
  d. Undefined

142. In mathematics, the additive inverse, or _____ of a number n is the number that, when added to n, yields zero. The additive inverse of n is denoted −n. For example, 7 is −7, because 7 + (−7) = 0, and the additive inverse of −0.3 is 0.3, because −0.3 + 0.3 = 0.
  a. Thing
  b. Opposite0
  c. Undefined
  d. Undefined

143. _____ is a subset of a population.
  a. Thing
  b. Sample0
  c. Undefined
  d. Undefined

144. In chemistry, a _____ is substance made by combining two or more different materials in such a way that no chemical reaction occurs.

## Chapter 5. Systems of Equations and Matrices 83

   a. Mixture0  
   c. Undefined  
   b. Thing  
   d. Undefined

145. _____ is a business term for the amount of money that a company receives from its activities in a given period, mostly from sales of products and/or services to customers
   a. Thing  
   c. Undefined  
   b. Revenue0  
   d. Undefined

146. _____ finance, in finance, a debt security, issued by Issuer
   a. Thing  
   c. Undefined  
   b. Bond0  
   d. Undefined

147. _____ is a form of periodic payment from an employer to an employee, which is specified in an employment contract.
   a. Thing  
   c. Undefined  
   b. Gross pay0  
   d. Undefined

148. _____ is the application of tools and a processing medium to the transformation of raw materials into finished goods for sale.
   a. Manufacturing0  
   c. Undefined  
   b. Thing  
   d. Undefined

149. A _____ is a form of periodic payment from an employer to an employee, which is specified in an employment contract.
   a. Thing  
   c. Undefined  
   b. Salary0  
   d. Undefined

150. _____ is a regression method that models the relationship between a dependent variable Y, independent variables Xp, and a random term å.
   a. Thing  
   c. Undefined  
   b. Linear regression0  
   d. Undefined

151. _____ is a mathematical science pertaining to the collection, analysis, interpretation or explanation, and presentation of data. It is applicable to a wide variety of academic disciplines, from the physical and social sciences to the humanities.
   a. Statistics0  
   c. Undefined  
   b. Thing  
   d. Undefined

152. In physics, _____ is an influence that may cause an object to accelerate. It may be experienced as a lift, a push, or a pull. The actual acceleration of the body is determined by the vector sum of all forces acting on it, known as net _____ or resultant _____.
   a. Thing  
   c. Undefined  
   b. Force0  
   d. Undefined

153. In economics _____ means before deductions brutto, e.g. _____ domestic or national product, or _____ profit or income

## Chapter 5. Systems of Equations and Matrices

a. Thing
b. Gross0
c. Undefined
d. Undefined

154. In _____ algebra, a *-ring is an associative ring with an antilinear, antiautomorphism * : A ¨ A which is an involution.
a. Star0
b. Thing
c. Undefined
d. Undefined

155. U.S. liquid _____ is legally defined as 231 cubic inches, and is equal to 3.785411784 litres or abotu 0.13368 cubic feet. This is the most common definition of a _____. The U.S. fluid ounce is defined as 1/128 of a U.S. _____.
a. Thing
b. Gallon0
c. Undefined
d. Undefined

156. In set theory and other branches of mathematics, the _____ of a collection of sets is the set that contains everything that belongs to any of the sets, but nothing else.
a. Thing
b. Union0
c. Undefined
d. Undefined

157. _____ is an adjective usually refering to being in the centre.
a. Thing
b. Central0
c. Undefined
d. Undefined

158. In botany, _____ are above-ground plant organs specialized for photosynthesis. Their characteristics are typically analyzed by using Fiobonacci's sequences.
a. Leaves0
b. Thing
c. Undefined
d. Undefined

159. _____ was a German mathematician and scientist of profound genius who contributed significantly to many fields, including number theory, analysis, differential geometry, geodesy, magnetism, astronomy, and optics.
a. Karl Friedrich Gauss0
b. Person
c. Undefined
d. Undefined

160. _____ is an algorithm which can be used to determine the solutions of a system of linear equations, to find the rank of a matrix, and to calculate the inverse of an invertible square matrix.
a. Thing
b. Gaussian elimination0
c. Undefined
d. Undefined

161. A _____ of a number is the product of that number with any integer.
a. Thing
b. Multiple0
c. Undefined
d. Undefined

162. In mathematics, a _____ is an n-tuple with n being 3.
a. Triple0
b. Thing
c. Undefined
d. Undefined

## Chapter 5. Systems of Equations and Matrices

163. In mathematics, a _____ is a two-dimensional manifold or surface that is perfectly flat.
   a. Thing
   b. Plane0
   c. Undefined
   d. Undefined

164. In mathematics, _____ are two-dimensional manifolds or surfaces that are perfectly flat.
   a. Thing
   b. Planes0
   c. Undefined
   d. Undefined

165. _____ is the design, analysis, and/or construction of works for practical purposes.
   a. Engineering0
   b. Thing
   c. Undefined
   d. Undefined

166. A _____ is a form of collective investment that pools money from many investors and invests their money in stocks, bonds, short-term money market instruments, and/or other securities.
   a. Thing
   b. Mutual fund0
   c. Undefined
   d. Undefined

167. A _____ is a polynomial function of the form $f(x) = ax^2 + bx + c$, where a, b, c are real numbers and a , 0.
   a. Quadratic function0
   b. Event
   c. Undefined
   d. Undefined

168. A _____ is an abstract model that uses mathematical language to describe the behavior of a system. Eykhoff defined a _____ as 'a representation of the essential aspects of an existing system which presents knowledge of that system in usable form'.
   a. Thing
   b. Mathematical model0
   c. Undefined
   d. Undefined

169. The _____ of a solid object is the three-dimensional concept of how much space it occupies, often quantified numerically.
   a. Thing
   b. Volume0
   c. Undefined
   d. Undefined

170. In geometry, an _____ angle is an angle that is not a 90 degree angle, or an angle that is divisible by 90: 180, 270, 360/0
   a. Thing
   b. Oblique0
   c. Undefined
   d. Undefined

171. In mathematics, a _____ is any function which can be written as the ratio of two polynomial functions.
   a. Rational function0
   b. Thing
   c. Undefined
   d. Undefined

172. _____ is often used to describe the measurement of the steepness, incline, gradient, or grade of a straight line. The _____ is defined as the ratio of the "rise" divided by the "run" between two points on a line, or in other words, the ratio of the altitude change to the horizontal distance between any two points on the line.

## Chapter 5. Systems of Equations and Matrices

a. Slope0  
b. Thing  
c. Undefined  
d. Undefined

173. In geometry, two lines or planes if one falls on the other in such a way as to create congruent adjacent angles. The term may be used as a noun or adjective. Thus, referring to Figure 1, the line AB is the _____ to CD through the point B.
  a. Perpendicular0  
  b. Thing  
  c. Undefined  
  d. Undefined

174. _____ is a branch of mathematics concerning the study of structure, relation and quantity.
  a. Concept  
  b. Algebra0  
  c. Undefined  
  d. Undefined

175. In mathematics, a _____ is a statement that can be proved on the basis of explicitly stated or previously agreed assumptions.
  a. Theorem0  
  b. Thing  
  c. Undefined  
  d. Undefined

176. _____ was a highly influential French philosopher, mathematician, scientist, and writer. Dubbed the "Founder of Modern Philosophy", and the "Father of Modern Mathematics". His theories provided the basis for the calculus of Newton and Leibniz, by applying infinitesimal calculus to the tangent line problem, thus permitting the evolution of that branch of modern mathematics
  a. Descartes0  
  b. Person  
  c. Undefined  
  d. Undefined

177. The _____ implies that on any great circle around the world, the temperature, pressure, elevation, carbon dioxide concentration, or anything else that varies continuously, there will always exist two antipodal points that share the same value for that variable.
  a. Thing  
  b. Intermediate Value Theorem0  
  c. Undefined  
  d. Undefined

178. In number theory, the _____ of arithmetic (or unique factorization theorem) states that every natural number greater than 1 can be written as a unique product of prime numbers.
  a. Fundamental theorem0  
  b. Concept  
  c. Undefined  
  d. Undefined

179. _____ states that every non-zero single-variable polynomial, with complex coefficients, has exactly as many complex roots as its degree, if repeated roots are counted up to their multiplicity.
  a. Fundamental theorem of algebra0  
  b. Thing  
  c. Undefined  
  d. Undefined

180. In mathematics and logic, a _____ proof is a way of showing the truth or falsehood of a given statement by a straightforward combination of established facts, usually existing lemmas and theorems, without making any further assumptions.
  a. Direct0  
  b. Thing  
  c. Undefined  
  d. Undefined

## Chapter 5. Systems of Equations and Matrices

181. _____ is the relationship between two variables, like a ratio in which the two quantities being compared are different units.
 a. Thing
 b. Direct variation0
 c. Undefined
 d. Undefined

182. In geometry, the _____ of an object is a point in some sense in the middle of the object.
 a. Thing
 b. Center0
 c. Undefined
 d. Undefined

183. In mathematics, a _____ is a rectangular table of numbers or, more generally, a table consisting of abstract quantities that can be added and multiplied.
 a. Matrix0
 b. Thing
 c. Undefined
 d. Undefined

184. In computer science an _____ is a data structure that consists of a group of elements having a single name that are accessed by indexing. In most programming languages each element has the same data type and the _____ occupies a continuous area of storage.
 a. Array0
 b. Thing
 c. Undefined
 d. Undefined

185. In linear algebra, the _____ of a matrix is obtained by combining two matrices in such a way that a matrix of coefficients to which has been added a column of constants corresponds to the right hand side of the equations.
 a. Augmented matrix0
 b. Thing
 c. Undefined
 d. Undefined

186. _____ is a fixed, but possibly unspecified, value. This is in contrast to a variable, which is not fixed.
 a. Constant term0
 b. Thing
 c. Undefined
 d. Undefined

187. In linear algebra, the _____ refers to a matrix consisting of the coefficients of the variables in a set of linear equations.
 a. Coefficient matrix0
 b. Thing
 c. Undefined
 d. Undefined

188. In mathematics, a matrix can be thought of as each row or _____ being a vector. Hence, a space formed by row vectors or _____ vectors are said to be a row space or a _____ space.
 a. Concept
 b. Column0
 c. Undefined
 d. Undefined

189. In linear algebra, the _____ of a square matrix is the diagonal which runs from the top left corner to the bottom right corner.
 a. Main diagonal0
 b. Thing
 c. Undefined
 d. Undefined

190. A _____ can refer to a line joining two nonadjacent vertices of a polygon or polyhedron, or in some contexts any upward or downward sloping line. .

a. Thing  
c. Undefined  
b. Diagonal0  
d. Undefined

191. A _____ is the sum of the elements of a sequence.
a. Thing  
c. Undefined  
b. Series0  
d. Undefined

192. In mathematics, a matrix is in row _____ if is satisfies the following requirements: • All nonzero rows are above any rows of all zeroes. • The leading coefficient of a row is always strictly to the right of the leading coefficient of the row above it.
a. Echelon form0  
c. Undefined  
b. Thing  
d. Undefined

193. A _____ is a number, figure, or indicator that appears below the normal line of type, typically used in a formula, mathematical expression, or description of a chemical compound.
a. Thing  
c. Undefined  
b. Subscript0  
d. Undefined

194. In mathematics, the _____ inverse, or opposite, of a number n is the number that, when added to n, yields zero. The _____ inverse of n is denoted −n.
a. Additive0  
c. Undefined  
b. Thing  
d. Undefined

195. In mathematics, the _____ of a number n is the number that, when added to n, yields zero. The _____ of n is denoted −n. For example, 7 is −7, because 7 + (−7) = 0, and the _____ of −0.3 is 0.3, because −0.3 + 0.3 = 0.
a. Additive inverse0  
c. Undefined  
b. Thing  
d. Undefined

196. In mathematics, particularly linear algebra, a _____ is a matrix with all its entries being zero.
a. Thing  
c. Undefined  
b. Zero matrix0  
d. Undefined

197. In linear algebra, real numbers are called scalars and relate to vectors in a vector space through the operation of _____ multiplication, in which a vector can be multiplied by a number to produce another vector.
a. Thing  
c. Undefined  
b. Scalar0  
d. Undefined

198. _____ is one of the basic operations defining a vector space in linear algebra.
a. Thing  
c. Undefined  
b. Scalar multiplication0  
d. Undefined

199. In mathematics, _____ is a property that a binary operation can have. Within an expression containing two or more of the same associative operators in a row, the order of operations does not matter as long as the sequence of the operands is not changed.

## Chapter 5. Systems of Equations and Matrices

a. Associativity0
b. Thing
c. Undefined
d. Undefined

200. An _____ is an equality that remains true regardless of the values of any variables that appear within it, to distinguish it from an equality which is true under more particular conditions.
a. Identity0
b. Thing
c. Undefined
d. Undefined

201. _____, from Latin meaning "to make progress", is defined in two different ways. Pure economic _____ is the increase in wealth that an investor has from making an investment, taking into consideration all costs associated with that investment including the opportunity cost of capital.
a. Thing
b. Profit0
c. Undefined
d. Undefined

202. In mathematics, the _____ inverse of a number x, denoted 1/x or $x^{-1}$, is the number which, when multiplied by x, yields 1. The _____ inverse of x is also called the reciprocal of x.
a. Multiplicative0
b. Thing
c. Undefined
d. Undefined

203. In mathematics, the idea of _____ generalises the concepts of negation, in relation to addition, and reciprocal, in relation to multiplication.
a. Inverse element0
b. Thing
c. Undefined
d. Undefined

204. In algebra, a _____ is a function depending on n that associates a scalar, det(A), to every n×n square matrix A.
a. Thing
b. Determinant0
c. Undefined
d. Undefined

205. In linear algebra, a _____ or minor of a matrix A is the determinant of some smaller square matrix, cut down from A.
a. Thing
b. Cofactor0
c. Undefined
d. Undefined

206. In linear algebra, a _____ of a matrix A is the determinant of some smaller square matrix, cut down from A.
a. Thing
b. Minor0
c. Undefined
d. Undefined

207. In mathematics, the _____, or members of a set or more generally a class are all those objects which when collected together make up the set or class.
a. Elements0
b. Thing
c. Undefined
d. Undefined

208. A _____ is a numeral used to indicate a count. The most common use of the word today is to name the part of a fraction that tells the number or count of equal parts.

## Chapter 5. Systems of Equations and Matrices

a. Numerator0  
b. Thing  
c. Undefined  
d. Undefined

209. A _____ is the part of a fraction that tells how many equal parts make up a whole, and which is used in the name of the fraction: "halves", "thirds", "fourths" or "quarters", "fifths" and so on.
   a. Concept
   b. Denominator0
   c. Undefined
   d. Undefined

210. In mathematics, _____ problems involve the optimization of a linear objective function, subject to linear equality and inequality constraints.
   a. Linear programming0
   b. Thing
   c. Undefined
   d. Undefined

211. In geometry a _____ is a plane figure that is bounded by a closed path or circuit, composed of a finite number of sequential line segments.
   a. Thing
   b. Polygon0
   c. Undefined
   d. Undefined

212. In mathematics, a _____ is a condition that a solution to an optimization problem must satisfy in order to be acceptable.
   a. Constraint0
   b. Thing
   c. Undefined
   d. Undefined

213. In mathematics, a _____ function in the sense of algebraic geometry is an everywhere-defined, polynomial function on an algebraic variety V with values in the field K over which V is defined.
   a. Regular0
   b. Thing
   c. Undefined
   d. Undefined

214. Transport or _____ is the movement of people and goods from one place to another.
   a. Transportation0
   b. Thing
   c. Undefined
   d. Undefined

215. In algebra, the _____ decomposition or _____ expansion is used to reduce the degree of either the numerator or the denominator of a rational function.
   a. Partial fraction0
   b. Thing
   c. Undefined
   d. Undefined

216. _____ is a mathematical subject that includes the study of limits, derivatives, integrals, and power series and constitutes a major part of modern university curriculum.
   a. Calculus0
   b. Thing
   c. Undefined
   d. Undefined

217. _____ refers to the reduction of the body of a formerly living organism into simpler forms of matter.
   a. Decomposing0
   b. Thing
   c. Undefined
   d. Undefined

## Chapter 5. Systems of Equations and Matrices

218. In mathematics, factorization (British English: factorisation) or factoring is the decomposition of an object (for example, a number, a polynomial, or a matrix) into a product of other objects, or _____, which when multiplied together give the original.
   a. Thing
   b. Factors0
   c. Undefined
   d. Undefined

219. The _____ is a property of multiplication or addition where the product or sum remains the same, regardless of whether or not the order of the addends or factors are changed.
   a. Thing
   b. Commutative property0
   c. Undefined
   d. Undefined

220. In mathematics the _____ of a set which is equipped with the operation of addition is an element which, when added to any other element x in the set, yields x.
   a. Additive identity0
   b. Concept
   c. Undefined
   d. Undefined

221. The _____ states that - a number and its additive inverse have a sum of zero (0).
   a. Additive inverse property0
   b. Concept
   c. Undefined
   d. Undefined

## Chapter 6. Conic Sections

1. _____ is the distance around a given two-dimensional object. As a general rule, the _____ of a polygon can always be calculated by adding all the length of the sides together. So, the formula for triangles is P = a + b + c, where a, b and c stand for each side of it. For quadrilaterals the equation is P = a + b + c + d. For equilateral polygons, P = na, where n is the number of sides and a is the side length.
   a. Perimeter0
   b. Thing
   c. Undefined
   d. Undefined

2. _____ is a three-dimensional geometric shape formed by straight lines through a fixed point vertex to the points of a fixed curve directrix.
   a. Thing
   b. Right circular cone0
   c. Undefined
   d. Undefined

3. In mathematics, a _____ is a two-dimensional manifold or surface that is perfectly flat.
   a. Plane0
   b. Thing
   c. Undefined
   d. Undefined

4. A _____ is a three-dimensional geometric shape formed by straight lines through a fixed point (vertex) to the points of a fixed curve (directrix)
   a. Concept
   b. Cone0
   c. Undefined
   d. Undefined

5. In mathematics, a _____ section is a curve that can be formed by intersecting a cone with a plane.
   a. Conic0
   b. Thing
   c. Undefined
   d. Undefined

6. In Euclidean geometry, a _____ is the set of all points in a plane at a fixed distance, called the radius, from a given point, the center.
   a. Thing
   b. Circle0
   c. Undefined
   d. Undefined

7. In mathematics, an _____ .
   a. Ellipse0
   b. Thing
   c. Undefined
   d. Undefined

8. In mathematics, the concept of a _____ tries to capture the intuitive idea of a geometrical one-dimensional and continuous object. A simple example is the circle.
   a. Curve0
   b. Thing
   c. Undefined
   d. Undefined

9. In mathematics, _____ are the intuitive idea of a geometrical one-dimensional and continuous object.
   a. Thing
   b. Curves0
   c. Undefined
   d. Undefined

10. In mathematics, the _____ is a conic section generated by the intersection of a right circular conical surface and a plane parallel to a generating straight line of that surface. It can also be defined as locus of points in a plane which are equidistant from a given point.

## Chapter 6. Conic Sections

a. Thing
c. Undefined
b. Parabola0
d. Undefined

11. In mathematics, a _____ is a type of conic section defined as the intersection between a right circular conical surface and a plane which cuts through both halves of the cone.
a. Thing
c. Undefined
b. Hyperbola0
d. Undefined

12. A _____ is a polynomial function of the form $f(x) = ax^2 + bx + c$, where a, b, c are real numbers and a , 0.
a. Event
c. Undefined
b. Quadratic function0
d. Undefined

13. The mathematical concept of a _____ expresses the intuitive idea of deterministic dependence between two quantities, one of which is viewed as primary and the other as secondary. A _____ then is a way to associate a unique output for each input of a specified type, for example, a real number or an element of a given set.
a. Function0
c. Undefined
b. Thing
d. Undefined

14. _____ means "constancy", i.e. if something retains a certain feature even after we change a way of looking at it, then it is symmetric.
a. Symmetry0
c. Undefined
b. Thing
d. Undefined

15. An _____ is a straight line around which a geometric figure can be rotated.
a. Axis0
c. Undefined
b. Thing
d. Undefined

16. _____ of a two-dimensional figure is a line such that, if a perpendicular is constructed, any two points lying on the perpendicular at equal distances from the _____ are identical.
a. Thing
c. Undefined
b. Axis of symmetry0
d. Undefined

17. In geometry, two lines or planes if one falls on the other in such a way as to create congruent adjacent angles. The term may be used as a noun or adjective. Thus, referring to Figure 1, the line AB is the _____ to CD through the point B.
a. Thing
c. Undefined
b. Perpendicular0
d. Undefined

18. In geometry, a line _____ is a part of a line that is bounded by two end points, and contains every point on the line between its end points.
a. Segment0
c. Undefined
b. Concept
d. Undefined

19. In geometry, a _____ is a special kind of point, usually a corner of a polygon, polyhedron, or higher dimensional polytope. In the geometry of curves a _____ is a point of where the first derivative of curvature is zero. In graph theory, a _____ is the fundamental unit out of which graphs are formed

## Chapter 6. Conic Sections

a. Vertex0  
c. Undefined  
b. Thing  
d. Undefined

20. _____ is the middle point of a line segment.
   a. Midpoint0
   b. Thing
   c. Undefined
   d. Undefined

21. A _____ is a set of numbers that designate location in a given reference system, such as x,y in a planar _____ system or an x,y,z in a three-dimensional _____ system.
   a. Thing
   b. Coordinate0
   c. Undefined
   d. Undefined

22. _____ is a notation for writing numbers that is often used by scientists and mathematicians to make it easier to write large and small numbers.
   a. Scientific notation0
   b. Thing
   c. Undefined
   d. Undefined

23. In elementary algebra, a _____ is a polynomial with two terms: the sum of two monomials. It is the simplest kind of polynomial except for a monomial.
   a. Binomial0
   b. Thing
   c. Undefined
   d. Undefined

24. _____ Logic is a concept in traditional logic referring to a "type of immediate inference in which from a given proposition another proposition is inferred which has as its subject the predicate of the original proposition and as its predicate the subject of the original proposition (the quality of the proposition being retained)."
   a. Concept
   b. Converse0
   c. Undefined
   d. Undefined

25. The _____ of measurement are a globally standardized and modernized form of the metric system.
   a. Units0
   b. Thing
   c. Undefined
   d. Undefined

26. In geometry, the _____ of an object is a point in some sense in the middle of the object.
   a. Thing
   b. Center0
   c. Undefined
   d. Undefined

27. In astronomy, geography, geometry and related sciences and contexts, a plane is said to be _____ at a given point if it is locally perpendicular to the gradient of the gravity field, i.e., with the direction of the gravitational force at that point.
   a. Horizontal0
   b. Thing
   c. Undefined
   d. Undefined

28. In plane geometry, a _____ is a polygon with four equal sides, four right angles, and parallel opposite sides. In algebra, the _____ of a number is that number multiplied by itself.
   a. Thing
   b. Square0
   c. Undefined
   d. Undefined

## Chapter 6. Conic Sections

29. A _____ is a negotiable instrument instructing a financial institution to pay a specific amount of a specific currency from a specific demand account held in the maker/depositor's name with that institution. Both the maker and payee may be natural persons or legal entities.
    a. Thing
    b. Check0
    c. Undefined
    d. Undefined

30. In mathematics, _____ is the decomposition of an object into a product of other objects, or factors, which when multiplied together give the original.
    a. Factoring0
    b. Thing
    c. Undefined
    d. Undefined

31. _____ is electromagnetic radiation with a wavelength that is visible to the eye (visible _____) or, in a technical or scientific context, electromagnetic radiation of any wavelength.
    a. Light0
    b. Thing
    c. Undefined
    d. Undefined

32. In geometry, a _____ is the intersection of a body in 2-dimensional space with a line, or of a body in 3-dimensional space with a plane
    a. Cross section0
    b. Thing
    c. Undefined
    d. Undefined

33. In probability theory, _____ are various sets of outcomes (a subset of the sample space) to which a probability is assigned.
    a. Thing
    b. Events0
    c. Undefined
    d. Undefined

34. Sound is a disturbance of mechanical energy that propagates through matter as a wave or _____.
    a. Sound wave0
    b. Thing
    c. Undefined
    d. Undefined

35. A _____ is a type of bridge that has been created since ancient times as early as 100 AD.
    a. Thing
    b. Suspension bridge0
    c. Undefined
    d. Undefined

36. _____ is the shape of a hanging flexible chain or cable when supported at its ends and acted upon by a uniform gravitational force. The chain is steepest near the points of suspension because this part of the chain has the most weight pulling down on it. Toward the bottom, the slope of the chain decreases because the chain is supporting less weight.
    a. Catenary0
    b. Thing
    c. Undefined
    d. Undefined

37. _____ are the basic objects of study in graph theory. Informally speaking, a graph is a set of objects called points, nodes, or vertices connected by links called lines or edges.
    a. Graphs0
    b. Thing
    c. Undefined
    d. Undefined

## Chapter 6. Conic Sections

38. In geometry, a _____ (Greek words diairo = divide and metro = measure) of a circle is any straight line segment that passes through the centre and whose endpoints are on the circular boundary, or, in more modern usage, the length of such a line segment. When using the word in the more modern sense, one speaks of the _____ rather than a _____, because all diameters of a circle have the same length. This length is twice the radius. The _____ of a circle is also the longest chord that the circle has.
    a. Diameter0
    b. Thing
    c. Undefined
    d. Undefined

39. In mathematics and its applications, a _____ is a system for assigning an n-tuple of numbers or scalars to each point in an n-dimensional space.
    a. Concept
    b. Coordinate system0
    c. Undefined
    d. Undefined

40. In mathematics, the _____ of a coordinate system is the point where the axes of the system intersect.
    a. Thing
    b. Origin0
    c. Undefined
    d. Undefined

41. In classical geometry, a _____ of a circle or sphere is any line segment from its center to its boundary. By extension, the _____ of a circle or sphere is the length of any such segment. The _____ is half the diameter. In science and engineering the term _____ of curvature is commonly used as a synonym for _____.
    a. Thing
    b. Radius0
    c. Undefined
    d. Undefined

42. In geometry, the _____ are a pair of special points used in describing conic sections. The four types of conic sections are the circle, parabola, ellipse, and hyperbola.
    a. Foci0
    b. Thing
    c. Undefined
    d. Undefined

43. A _____ signifies a point or points of probability on a subject e.g., the _____ of creativity, which allows for the formation of rule or norm or law by interpretation of the phenomena events that can be created.
    a. Thing
    b. Principle0
    c. Undefined
    d. Undefined

44. A quadratic equation with real solutions, called roots, which may be real or complex, is given by the _____: $x = \frac{-b \pm \sqrt{b^2 - 4ac}}{2a}$.
    a. Quadratic formula0
    b. Thing
    c. Undefined
    d. Undefined

45. In mathematics, a _____ of a number x is a number r such that $r^2 = x$, or in words, a number r whose square (the result of multiplying the number by itself) is x.
    a. Square root0
    b. Thing
    c. Undefined
    d. Undefined

46. In mathematics, a _____ of a complex-valued function f is a member x of the domain of f such that f(x) vanishes at x, that is, $x : f(x) = 0$.

## Chapter 6. Conic Sections

a. Root0  
b. Thing  
c. Undefined  
d. Undefined  

47. In geographic information systems, a _____ comprises an entity with a geographic location, typically determined by points, arcs, or polygons. Carriageways and cadastres exemplify _____ data.
   a. Feature0  
   b. Thing  
   c. Undefined  
   d. Undefined  

48. A _____ is 360° or 2∂ radians.
   a. Thing  
   b. Turn0  
   c. Undefined  
   d. Undefined  

49. A _____ is the result of the addition of a set of numbers. The numbers may be natural numbers, complex numbers, matrices, or still more complicated objects. An infinite _____ is a subtle procedure known as a series.
   a. Sum0  
   b. Thing  
   c. Undefined  
   d. Undefined  

50. In mathematics and the mathematical sciences, a _____ is a fixed, but possibly unspecified, value. This is in contrast to a variable, which is not fixed.
   a. Thing  
   b. Constant0  
   c. Undefined  
   d. Undefined  

51. In linear algebra, a _____ of a matrix A is the determinant of some smaller square matrix, cut down from A.
   a. Thing  
   b. Minor0  
   c. Undefined  
   d. Undefined  

52. _____ is a technique used in algebra to solve quadratic equations, in analytic geometry for determining the shapes of graphs, and in calculus for computing integrals, including, but hardly limited to, the integrals that define Laplace transforms. The essential objective is to reduce a quadratic polynomial in a variable in an equation or expression to a squared polynomial of linear order. This can reduce an equation or integral to one that is more easily solved or evaluated.
   a. Thing  
   b. Completing the square0  
   c. Undefined  
   d. Undefined  

53. A _____ is a special kind of ratio, indicating a relationship between two measurements with different units, such as miles to gallons or cents to pounds.
   a. Rate0  
   b. Thing  
   c. Undefined  
   d. Undefined  

54. A _____ is a gallery beneath a dome or vault or enclosed in a circular or elliptical area in which whispers can be heard clearly in other parts of the building.
   a. Whispering gallery0  
   b. Thing  
   c. Undefined  
   d. Undefined  

55. _____ is the transport of people on a trip/journey or the process or time involved in a person or object moving from one location to another.

a. Travel0  
b. Thing  
c. Undefined  
d. Undefined  

56. In physics, an _____ is the path that an object makes around another object while under the influence of a source of centripetal force, such as gravity.
   a. Thing  
   b. Orbit0  
   c. Undefined  
   d. Undefined  

57. In the context of spaceflight, a _____ are any object which has been placed into orbit by human endeavor.
   a. Satellites0  
   b. Thing  
   c. Undefined  
   d. Undefined  

58. A _____, as defined by the International Astronomical Union, is a celestial body orbiting a star or stellar remnant that is massive enough to be rounded by its own gravity, not massive enough to cause thermonuclear fusion in its core, and has cleared its neighboring region of planetesimals.
   a. Thing  
   b. Planet0  
   c. Undefined  
   d. Undefined  

59. _____ is a parameter associated with every conic section.
   a. Eccentricity0  
   b. Thing  
   c. Undefined  
   d. Undefined  

60. An _____ is when two lines intersect somewhere on a plane creating a right angle at intersection
   a. Axes0  
   b. Thing  
   c. Undefined  
   d. Undefined  

61. In mathematics, a _____ is a polynomial equation of the second degree. The general form is $ax^2 + bx + c = 0$.
   a. Thing  
   b. Quadratic equation0  
   c. Undefined  
   d. Undefined  

62. In mathematics, an _____ number is a complex number whose square is a negative real number. They were defined in 1572 by Rafael Bombelli.
   a. Thing  
   b. Imaginary0  
   c. Undefined  
   d. Undefined  

63. The word _____ comes from the Latin word linearis, which means created by lines.
   a. Thing  
   b. Linear0  
   c. Undefined  
   d. Undefined  

64. A _____ is an equation in which each term is either a constant or the product of a constant times the first power of a variable.
   a. Linear equation0  
   b. Thing  
   c. Undefined  
   d. Undefined  

65. A _____ defined function $f(x)$ of a real variable $x$ is a function whose definition is given differently on disjoint subsets of its domain.

## Chapter 6. Conic Sections

a. Piecewise0  
b. Thing  
c. Undefined  
d. Undefined

66. A _____ is the part of the dividend that is left over when the dividend is not evenly divisible by the divisor.
a. Remainder0  
b. Thing  
c. Undefined  
d. Undefined

67. In mathematics, a _____ is an expression that is constructed from one or more variables and constants, using only the operations of addition, subtraction, multiplication, and constant positive whole number exponents. is a _____. Note in particular that division by an expression containing a variable is not in general allowed in polynomials. [1]
a. Thing  
b. Polynomial0  
c. Undefined  
d. Undefined

68. In geometry, an _____ is a point at which a line segment or ray terminates.
a. Thing  
b. Endpoint0  
c. Undefined  
d. Undefined

69. In mathematics, the _____ (or modulus) of a real number is its numerical value without regard to its sign.
a. Absolute value0  
b. Thing  
c. Undefined  
d. Undefined

70. In algebra, a _____ is a binomial formed by taking the opposite of the second term of a binomial.
a. Thing  
b. Conjugate0  
c. Undefined  
d. Undefined

71. An _____ is a straight line or curve A to which another curve B approaches closer and closer as one moves along it. As one moves along B, the space between it and the _____ A becomes smaller and smaller, and can in fact be made as small as one could wish by going far enough along. A curve may or may not touch or cross its _____. In fact, the curve may intersect the _____ an infinite number of times.
a. Thing  
b. Asymptote0  
c. Undefined  
d. Undefined

72. A _____ can refer to a line joining two nonadjacent vertices of a polygon or polyhedron, or in some contexts any upward or downward sloping line. .
a. Thing  
b. Diagonal0  
c. Undefined  
d. Undefined

73. A _____ is a symbolic representation denoting a quantity or expression. It often represents an "unknown" quantity that has the potential to change.
a. Variable0  
b. Thing  
c. Undefined  
d. Undefined

74. Equivalence is the condition of being _____ or essentially equal.
a. Thing  
b. Equivalent0  
c. Undefined  
d. Undefined

## Chapter 6. Conic Sections

75. In mathematics, a _____ is a constant multiplicative factor of a certain object. The object can be such things as a variable, a vector, a function, etc. For example, the _____ of $9x^2$ is 9.
   a. Coefficient0
   b. Thing
   c. Undefined
   d. Undefined

76. _____ is the process of planning, recording, and controlling the movement of a craft or vehicle from one place to another.
   a. Thing
   b. Navigation0
   c. Undefined
   d. Undefined

77. _____ is the property of two events happening at the same time in at least one reference frame.
   a. Thing
   b. Simultaneous0
   c. Undefined
   d. Undefined

78. In mathematics, the conjugate _____ or adjoint matrix of an m-by-n matrix A with complex entries is the n-by-m matrix A* obtained from A by taking the transpose and then taking the complex conjugate of each entry.
   a. Pairs0
   b. Thing
   c. Undefined
   d. Undefined

79. In mathematics, the _____ of two sets A and B is the set that contains all elements of A that also belong to B (or equivalently, all elements of B that also belong to A), but no other elements.
   a. Intersection0
   b. Thing
   c. Undefined
   d. Undefined

80. A _____ is a unit of length, usually used to measure distance, in a number of different systems, including Imperial units, United States customary units and Norwegian/Swedish mil. Its size can vary from system to system, but in each is between 1 and 10 kilometers. In contemporary English contexts _____ refers to either:
   a. Thing
   b. Mile0
   c. Undefined
   d. Undefined

81. _____ systems represent systems whose behavior is not expressible as a sum of the behaviors of its descriptors.
   a. Nonlinear0
   b. Thing
   c. Undefined
   d. Undefined

82. A _____ represents a system whose behavior is not expressible as a sum of the behaviors of its descriptors.
   a. Thing
   b. Nonlinear system0
   c. Undefined
   d. Undefined

83. _____ are a set of equations containing multiple variables.
   a. Systems of equations0
   b. Thing
   c. Undefined
   d. Undefined

84. The Gaussian _____ is an algorithm which can be used to determine the solutions of a system of linear equations, to find the rank of a matrix, and to calculate the inverse of an invertible square matrix.

a. Thing
b. Elimination method0
c. Undefined
d. Undefined

85. The _____ is used to discard one of the variables in an equation, only to replace it with the actual value when solving multiple equations.
a. Substitution method0
b. Thing
c. Undefined
d. Undefined

86. An _____ is a collection of two not necessarily distinct objects, one of which is distinguished as the first coordinate and the other as the second coordinate.
a. Thing
b. Ordered pair0
c. Undefined
d. Undefined

87. _____ forms part of thinking. Considered the most complex of all intellectual functions, _____ has been defined as higher-order cognitive process that requires the modulation and control of more routine or fundamental skills.
a. Thing
b. Problem solving0
c. Undefined
d. Undefined

88. Acid _____ ratio measures the ability of a company to use its near cash or quick assets to immediately extinguish its current liabilities.
a. Thing
b. Test0
c. Undefined
d. Undefined

89. _____ is the fee paid on borrowed money.
a. Thing
b. Interest0
c. Undefined
d. Undefined

90. _____ or investing is a term with several closely-related meanings in business management, finance and economics, related to saving or deferring consumption.
a. Thing
b. Investment0
c. Undefined
d. Undefined

91. An _____ is the fee paid on borrow money.
a. Interest rate0
b. Concept
c. Undefined
d. Undefined

92. In geometry, a _____ is defined as a quadrilateral where all four of its angles are right angles.
a. Rectangle0
b. Thing
c. Undefined
d. Undefined

93. The _____ is that number multiplied by itself.
a. Thing
b. Square of a number0
c. Undefined
d. Undefined

94. The _____ of a solid object is the three-dimensional concept of how much space it occupies, often quantified numerically.

a. Thing
b. Volume0
c. Undefined
d. Undefined

95. In mathematics, a _____ is the result of multiplying, or an expression that identifies factors to be multiplied.
  a. Product0
  b. Thing
  c. Undefined
  d. Undefined

96. A _____ is a three-dimensional solid object bounded by six square faces, facets, or sides, with three meeting at each vertex.
  a. Thing
  b. Cube0
  c. Undefined
  d. Undefined

97. _____ are of a number n in its third power-the result of multiplying it by itself three times.
  a. Thing
  b. Cubes0
  c. Undefined
  d. Undefined

98. In mathematics, the multiplicative inverse of a number x, denoted $1/x$ or $x^{-1}$, is the number which, when multiplied by x, yields 1. The multiplicative inverse of x is also called the _____ of x.
  a. Reciprocal0
  b. Thing
  c. Undefined
  d. Undefined

## Chapter 7. Sequences, Series, and Combinatorics

1. A _____ is the sum of the elements of a sequence.
   a. Thing
   b. Series0
   c. Undefined
   d. Undefined

2. Mathematical _____ is used to represent ideas.
   a. Notation0
   b. Thing
   c. Undefined
   d. Undefined

3. In mathematics, a _____ is an ordered list of objects. Like a set, it contains members, also called elements or terms, and the number of terms is called the length of the _____. Unlike a set, order matters, and the exact same elements can appear multiple times at different positions in the _____.
   a. Sequence0
   b. Thing
   c. Undefined
   d. Undefined

4. _____ is the state of being greater than any finite real or natural number, however large.
   a. Thing
   b. Infinite0
   c. Undefined
   d. Undefined

5. The _____ are the only integral domain whose positive elements are well-ordered, and in which order is preserved by addition. Like the natural numbers, the _____ form a countably infinite set. The set of all _____ is usually denoted in mathematics by a boldface Z .
   a. Thing
   b. Integers0
   c. Undefined
   d. Undefined

6. _____ is a kind of property which exists as magnitude or multitude. It is among the basic classes of things along with quality, substance, change, and relation.
   a. Thing
   b. Amount0
   c. Undefined
   d. Undefined

7. _____ means in succession or back-to-back
   a. Consecutive0
   b. Thing
   c. Undefined
   d. Undefined

8. The mathematical concept of a _____ expresses the intuitive idea of deterministic dependence between two quantities, one of which is viewed as primary and the other as secondary. A _____ then is a way to associate a unique output for each input of a specified type, for example, a real number or an element of a given set.
   a. Thing
   b. Function0
   c. Undefined
   d. Undefined

9. In mathematics, a _____ of a k-place relation $L \subseteq X_1 \times ... \times X_k$ is one of the sets $X_j$, $1 \le j \le k$. In the special case where k = 2 and $L \subseteq X_1 \times X_2$ is a function $L : X_1 \to X_2$, it is conventional to refer to $X_1$ as the _____ of the function and to refer to $X_2$ as the codomain of the function.
   a. Domain0
   b. Thing
   c. Undefined
   d. Undefined

10. In mathematics, a set is called _____ if there is a bijection between the set and some set of the form {1, 2, ..., n} where n is a natural number.

## Chapter 7. Sequences, Series, and Combinatorics

    a. Finite0  
    c. Undefined  
    b. Thing  
    d. Undefined

11. A _____ is a statement or claimt that a particular event will occur in the future in more certain terms than a forecast.
    a. Thing  
    c. Undefined  
    b. Prediction0  
    d. Undefined

12. In plane geometry, a _____ is a polygon with four equal sides, four right angles, and parallel opposite sides. In algebra, the _____ of a number is that number multiplied by itself.
    a. Square0  
    c. Undefined  
    b. Thing  
    d. Undefined

13. In mathematics, a _____ of a number x is a number r such that $r^2 = x$, or in words, a number r whose square (the result of multiplying the number by itself) is x.
    a. Thing  
    c. Undefined  
    b. Square root0  
    d. Undefined

14. In mathematics, a _____ of a complex-valued function f is a member x of the domain of f such that f(x) vanishes at x, that is, $x : f(x) = 0$.
    a. Root0  
    c. Undefined  
    b. Thing  
    d. Undefined

15. A _____ is the result of the addition of a set of numbers. The numbers may be natural numbers, complex numbers, matrices, or still more complicated objects. An infinite _____ is a subtle procedure known as a series.
    a. Sum0  
    c. Undefined  
    b. Thing  
    d. Undefined

16. _____ is often represented as the sum of a sequence of terms.
    a. Thing  
    c. Undefined  
    b. Infinite series0  
    d. Undefined

17. In statistics, _____ means the most frequent value assumed by a random variable, or occurring in a sampling of a random variable.
    a. Concept  
    c. Undefined  
    b. Mode0  
    d. Undefined

18. _____ is the eighteenth letter of the Greek alphabet.
    a. Thing  
    c. Undefined  
    b. Sigma0  
    d. Undefined

19. _____ is used as the symbol for summation. Summation is the addition of a set of numbers; the result is their sum. The "numbers" to be summed may be natural numbers, complex numbers, matrices, or still more complicated objects. An infinite sum is a subtle procedure known as a series.

## Chapter 7. Sequences, Series, and Combinatorics

a. Sigma notation0  
b. Thing  
c. Undefined  
d. Undefined

20. _____ is the addition of a set of numbers; the result is their sum. The "numbers" to be summed may be natural numbers, complex numbers, matrices, or still more complicated objects. An infinite sum is a subtle procedure known as a series.
    a. Summation0  
    b. Thing  
    c. Undefined  
    d. Undefined

21. The word _____ is used in a variety of ways in mathematics.
    a. Index0  
    b. Thing  
    c. Undefined  
    d. Undefined

22. _____ has many meanings, most of which simply .
    a. Power0  
    b. Thing  
    c. Undefined  
    d. Undefined

23. _____ is the fee paid on borrowed money.
    a. Interest0  
    b. Thing  
    c. Undefined  
    d. Undefined

24. _____ interest refers to the fact that whenever interest is calculated, it is based not only on the original principal, but also on any unpaid interest that has been added to the principal.
    a. Compound0  
    b. Thing  
    c. Undefined  
    d. Undefined

25. _____ refers to the fact that whenever interest is calculated, it is based not only on the original principal, but also on any unpaid interest that has been added to the principal. The more frequently interest is compounded, the faster the balance grows.
    a. Concept  
    b. Compound interest0  
    c. Undefined  
    d. Undefined

26. _____ or investing is a term with several closely-related meanings in business management, finance and economics, related to saving or deferring consumption.
    a. Thing  
    b. Investment0  
    c. Undefined  
    d. Undefined

27. In business, particularly accounting, a _____ is the time intervals that the accounts, statement, payments, or other calculations cover.
    a. Period0  
    b. Thing  
    c. Undefined  
    d. Undefined

28. _____ is a form of periodic payment from an employer to an employee, which is specified in an employment contract.

## Chapter 7. Sequences, Series, and Combinatorics

    a. Gross pay0  
    c. Undefined  
    b. Thing  
    d. Undefined

29. A _____ is a form of periodic payment from an employer to an employee, which is specified in an employment contract.
    a. Salary0  
    c. Undefined  
    b. Thing  
    d. Undefined

30. Leonardo of Pisa (1170s or 1180s – 1250), also known as Leonardo Pisano, Leonardo Bonacci, Leonardo _____, or, most commonly, simply _____, was an Italian mathematician, considered by some "the most talented mathematician of the Middle Ages."
    a. Person  
    c. Undefined  
    b. Fibonacci0  
    d. Undefined

31. In sociology and biology a _____ is the collection of people or organisms of a particular species living in a given geographic area or space, usually measured by a census.
    a. Population0  
    c. Undefined  
    b. Thing  
    d. Undefined

32. _____ is change in population over time, and can be quantified as the change in the number of individuals in a population per unit time.
    a. Population growth0  
    c. Undefined  
    b. Thing  
    d. Undefined

33. In mathematics, the conjugate _____ or adjoint matrix of an m-by-n matrix A with complex entries is the n-by-m matrix A* obtained from A by taking the transpose and then taking the complex conjugate of each entry.
    a. Pairs0  
    c. Undefined  
    b. Thing  
    d. Undefined

34. _____ is a synonym for information.
    a. Thing  
    c. Undefined  
    b. Data0  
    d. Undefined

35. In probability theory and statistics, a _____ is a number dividing the higher half of a sample, a population, or a probability distribution from the lower half.
    a. Concept  
    c. Undefined  
    b. Median0  
    d. Undefined

36. _____ or arithmetics is the oldest and most elementary branch of mathematics, used by almost everyone, for tasks ranging from simple daily counting to advanced science and business calculations.
    a. Arithmetic0  
    c. Undefined  
    b. Thing  
    d. Undefined

37. _____ is a sequence of numbers such that the difference of any two successive members of the sequence is a constant.

## Chapter 7. Sequences, Series, and Combinatorics

    a. Thing
    c. Undefined
    b. Arithmetic sequence0
    d. Undefined

38. A _____ is a number, figure, or indicator that appears below the normal line of type, typically used in a formula, mathematical expression, or description of a chemical compound.
    a. Subscript0
    c. Undefined
    b. Thing
    d. Undefined

39. In mathematics, a _____ is a constant multiplicative factor of a certain object. The object can be such things as a variable, a vector, a function, etc. For example, the _____ of $9x^2$ is 9.
    a. Coefficient0
    c. Undefined
    b. Thing
    d. Undefined

40. In mathematics, _____ are used in a variety of notations, including standard notations for intervals, commutators, the Lie bracket, and the Iverson bracket.
    a. Thing
    c. Undefined
    b. Square Brackets0
    d. Undefined

41. An _____ is a combination of numbers, operators, grouping symbols and/or free variables and bound variables arranged in a meaningful way which can be evaluated..
    a. Thing
    c. Undefined
    b. Expression0
    d. Undefined

42. In mathematics, a _____ can mean either an element of the set {1, 2, 3, ...} (i.e the positive integers or the counting numbers) or an element of the set {0, 1, 2, 3, ...} (i.e. the non-negative integers).
    a. Natural number0
    c. Undefined
    b. Thing
    d. Undefined

43. A _____ is a compensation which workers receive in exchange for their labor.
    a. Thing
    c. Undefined
    b. Wage0
    d. Undefined

44. A _____ is a special kind of ratio, indicating a relationship between two measurements with different units, such as miles to gallons or cents to pounds.
    a. Rate0
    c. Undefined
    b. Thing
    d. Undefined

45. A _____ is a deliberate process for transforming one or more inputs into one or more results.
    a. Calculation0
    c. Undefined
    b. Thing
    d. Undefined

46. A _____ of a number is the product of that number with any integer.
    a. Thing
    c. Undefined
    b. Multiple0
    d. Undefined

47. A _____ is a quadrilateral, which is defined as a shape with four sides, which has a pair of parallel sides.

## Chapter 7. Sequences, Series, and Combinatorics

a. Trapezoid0  
b. Thing  
c. Undefined  
d. Undefined

48. In mathematics, a _____ is the result of multiplying, or an expression that identifies factors to be multiplied.
   a. Product0  
   b. Thing  
   c. Undefined  
   d. Undefined

49. The _____ of measurement are a globally standardized and modernized form of the metric system.
   a. Units0  
   b. Thing  
   c. Undefined  
   d. Undefined

50. In mathematics, a _____ is an expression that is constructed from one or more variables and constants, using only the operations of addition, subtraction, multiplication, and constant positive whole number exponents. is a _____. Note in particular that division by an expression containing a variable is not in general allowed in polynomials. [1]
   a. Polynomial0  
   b. Thing  
   c. Undefined  
   d. Undefined

51. _____ of a list of numbers is the sum of all the members of the list divided by the number of items in the list.
   a. Thing  
   b. Arithmetic mean0  
   c. Undefined  
   d. Undefined

52. In mathematics, an _____, mean, or central tendency of a data set refers to a measure of the "middle" or "expected" value of the data set.
   a. Concept  
   b. Average0  
   c. Undefined  
   d. Undefined

53. The _____, the average in everyday English, which is also called the arithmetic _____ (and is distinguished from the geometric _____ or harmonic _____). The average is also called the sample _____. The expected value of a random variable, which is also called the population _____.
   a. Mean0  
   b. Thing  
   c. Undefined  
   d. Undefined

54. A _____ is a sequence of numbers where each term after the first is found by multiplying the previous one by a fixed non-zero number called the common ratio.
   a. Thing  
   b. Geometric sequence0  
   c. Undefined  
   d. Undefined

55. A _____ is a quantity that denotes the proportional amount or magnitude of one quantity relative to another.
   a. Thing  
   b. Ratio0  
   c. Undefined  
   d. Undefined

56. _____ is the income from capital investment paid in a series of regular payments.
   a. Thing  
   b. Annuity0  
   c. Undefined  
   d. Undefined

## Chapter 7. Sequences, Series, and Combinatorics

57. In elementary algebra, an _____ is a set that contains every real number between two indicated numbers and may contain the two numbers themselves.
   a. Thing
   b. Interval0
   c. Undefined
   d. Undefined

58. A _____ are accounts maintained by commercial banks, savings and loan associations, credit unions, and mutual savings banks that pay interest but can not be used directly as money by, for example, writing a cheque.
   a. Thing
   b. Savings account0
   c. Undefined
   d. Undefined

59. Initial objects are also called _____, and terminal objects are also called final.
   a. Thing
   b. Coterminal0
   c. Undefined
   d. Undefined

60. In common philosophical language, a proposition or _____, is the content of an assertion, that is, it is true-or-false and defined by the meaning of a particular piece of language.
   a. Concept
   b. Statement0
   c. Undefined
   d. Undefined

61. _____ are objects, characters, or other concrete representations of ideas, concepts, or other abstractions.
   a. Symbols0
   b. Thing
   c. Undefined
   d. Undefined

62. In mathematics, a _____ is a demonstration that, assuming certain axioms, some statement is necessarily true.
   a. Proof0
   b. Thing
   c. Undefined
   d. Undefined

63. _____ is a method of mathematical proof typically used to establish that a given statement is true of all natural numbers
   a. Thing
   b. Mathematical induction0
   c. Undefined
   d. Undefined

64. Mathematical _____ are demonstrations that,assuming certain axioms, some statement is necessarily true.
   a. Thing
   b. Proofs0
   c. Undefined
   d. Undefined

65. _____ is a mathematical operation, written $a^n$, involving two numbers, the base a and the exponent n.
   a. Exponentiating0
   b. Thing
   c. Undefined
   d. Undefined

66. _____ is a mathematical operation, written $a^n$, involving two numbers, the base a and the exponent n.
   a. Thing
   b. Exponentiation0
   c. Undefined
   d. Undefined

67. In geometry a _____ is a plane figure that is bounded by a closed path or circuit, composed of a finite number of sequential line segments.

a. Polygon0  
b. Thing  
c. Undefined  
d. Undefined  

68. A _____ can refer to a line joining two nonadjacent vertices of a polygon or polyhedron, or in some contexts any upward or downward sloping line. .  
a. Thing  
b. Diagonal0  
c. Undefined  
d. Undefined  

69. In mathematics, an inequality is a statement about the relative size or order of two objects. For example 14 > 10, or 14 is _____ 10.  
a. Greater than0  
b. Thing  
c. Undefined  
d. Undefined  

70. In mathematics, a _____ may be described informally as a number that can be given by an infinite decimal representation.  
a. Thing  
b. Real number0  
c. Undefined  
d. Undefined  

71. _____ of a non-negative integer n is the product of all positive integers less than or equal to n.  
a. Thing  
b. Factorial0  
c. Undefined  
d. Undefined  

72. _____ is the chance that something is likely to happen or be the case.  
a. Probability0  
b. Thing  
c. Undefined  
d. Undefined  

73. _____ is the mathematical action of repeatedly adding or subtracting one, usually to find out how many objects there are or to set aside a desired number of objects.  
a. Counting0  
b. Thing  
c. Undefined  
d. Undefined  

74. _____ is a branch of pure mathematics concerning the study of discrete objects. It is related to many other areas of mathematics, such as algebra, probability theory, ergodic theory and geometry, as well as to applied subjects such as computer science and statistical physics.  
a. Thing  
b. Combinatorics0  
c. Undefined  
d. Undefined  

75. _____ is the rearrangement of objects or symbols into distinguishable sequences.  
a. Thing  
b. Permutation0  
c. Undefined  
d. Undefined  

76. In mathematics, a _____ is a mathematical statement which appears likely to be true, but has not been formally proven to be true under the rules of mathematical logic.  
a. Conjecture0  
b. Concept  
c. Undefined  
d. Undefined

## Chapter 7. Sequences, Series, and Combinatorics

77. A _____ signifies a point or points of probability on a subject e.g., the _____ of creativity, which allows for the formation of rule or norm or law by interpretation of the phenomena events that can be created.
    a. Thing
    b. Principle0
    c. Undefined
    d. Undefined

78. The _____ is a method that is used to calculate all of the possibilities of a pertaining number of events.
    a. Fundamental Counting Principle0
    b. Thing
    c. Undefined
    d. Undefined

79. _____ the expected value of a random variable displays the average or central value of the variable. It is a summary value of the distribution of the variable.
    a. Thing
    b. Determining0
    c. Undefined
    d. Undefined

80. _____ primarily refers to social welfare service concerned with social protection, or protection against socially recognized conditions, including poverty, old age, disability, unemployment, families with children and others.
    a. Social security0
    b. Thing
    c. Undefined
    d. Undefined

81. _____ are activities that are governed by a set of rules or customs and often engaged in competitively.
    a. Thing
    b. Sports0
    c. Undefined
    d. Undefined

82. In combinatorial mathematics, a _____ is an un-ordered collection of unique elements.
    a. Combination0
    b. Concept
    c. Undefined
    d. Undefined

83. A _____ is a set whose members are members of another set or a set contained within another set.
    a. Subset0
    b. Thing
    c. Undefined
    d. Undefined

84. _____ are groups whose members are members of another set or a set contained within another set.
    a. Subsets0
    b. Thing
    c. Undefined
    d. Undefined

85. An _____ or member of a set is an object that when collected together make up the set.
    a. Thing
    b. Element0
    c. Undefined
    d. Undefined

86. In mathematics, the _____ , or members of a set or more generally a class are all those objects which when collected together make up the set or class.
    a. Elements0
    b. Thing
    c. Undefined
    d. Undefined

87. In elementary algebra, a _____ is a polynomial with two terms: the sum of two monomials. It is the simplest kind of polynomial except for a monomial.

## Chapter 7. Sequences, Series, and Combinatorics

a. Binomial0  
b. Thing  
c. Undefined  
d. Undefined

88. In mathematics, particularly in combinatorics, the _____ of the natural number n and the integer k is the number of combinations that exist.
   a. Binomial coefficient0
   b. Thing
   c. Undefined
   d. Undefined

89. _____ is the study of terms and their use — of words and compound words that are used in specific contexts.
   a. Thing
   b. Terminology0
   c. Undefined
   d. Undefined

90. A _____ is a numeral used to indicate a count. The most common use of the word today is to name the part of a fraction that tells the number or count of equal parts.
   a. Thing
   b. Numerator0
   c. Undefined
   d. Undefined

91. In mathematics, factorization (British English: factorisation) or factoring is the decomposition of an object (for example, a number, a polynomial, or a matrix) into a product of other objects, or _____, which when multiplied together give the original.
   a. Factors0
   b. Thing
   c. Undefined
   d. Undefined

92. The _____ is a popular form of gambling which involves the drawing of lots for a prize. Some governments forbid it, while others endorse it to the extent of organizign a national _____.
   a. Thing
   b. Lottery0
   c. Undefined
   d. Undefined

93. _____ are a measure of time.
   a. Minutes0
   b. Thing
   c. Undefined
   d. Undefined

94. Acid _____ ratio measures the ability of a company to use its near cash or quick assets to immediately extinguish its current liabilities.
   a. Test0
   b. Thing
   c. Undefined
   d. Undefined

95. The deductive-nomological model is a formalized view of scientific _____ in natural language.
   a. Explanation0
   b. Thing
   c. Undefined
   d. Undefined

96. In Euclidean geometry, a _____ is the set of all points in a plane at a fixed distance, called the radius, from a given point, the center.
   a. Thing
   b. Circle0
   c. Undefined
   d. Undefined

## Chapter 7. Sequences, Series, and Combinatorics

97. A _____ is one of the basic shapes of geometry: a polygon with three vertices and three sides which are straight line segments.
   a. Thing
   b. Triangle0
   c. Undefined
   d. Undefined

98. In mathematics, the _____ is an important formula giving the expansion of powers of sums.
   a. Binomial Theorem0
   b. Thing
   c. Undefined
   d. Undefined

99. Blaise _____ was a French mathematician, physicist, and religious philosopher.
   a. Person
   b. Pascal0
   c. Undefined
   d. Undefined

100. In mathematics, a _____ is a statement that can be proved on the basis of explicitly stated or previously agreed assumptions.
   a. Thing
   b. Theorem0
   c. Undefined
   d. Undefined

101. An _____ of a product of sums expresses it as a sum of products by using the fact that multiplication distributes over addition.
   a. Expansion0
   b. Thing
   c. Undefined
   d. Undefined

102. _____ was a French mathematician, physicist, and religious philosopher.
   a. Person
   b. Blaise Pascal0
   c. Undefined
   d. Undefined

103. In mathematics, the word _____ is used informally to refer to certain distinct bodies of knowledge about mathematics.
   a. Theoretical0
   b. Thing
   c. Undefined
   d. Undefined

104. _____ is the branch of mathematics concerned with analysis of random phenomena. The central objects of theoretical probabiltiy are random variables, stochastic processes, and events: mathematical abstractions of non-deterministic events or measured quantities that may either be single occurrences or evolve over time in an apparently random fashion.
   a. Theoretical probability0
   b. Thing
   c. Undefined
   d. Undefined

105. Deductive _____ is the kind of _____ in which the conclusion is necessitated by, or reached from, previously known facts (the premises).
   a. Thing
   b. Reasoning0
   c. Undefined
   d. Undefined

## Chapter 7. Sequences, Series, and Combinatorics

106. In the scientific method, an _____ (Latin: ex-+-periri, "of (or from) trying"), is a set of actions and observations, performed in the context of solving a particular problem or question, in order to support or falsify a hypothesis or research concerning phenomena.
   a. Thing
   b. Experiment0
   c. Undefined
   d. Undefined

107. A _____ is a negotiable instrument instructing a financial institution to pay a specific amount of a specific currency from a specific demand account held in the maker/depositor's name with that institution. Both the maker and payee may be natural persons or legal entities.
   a. Thing
   b. Check0
   c. Undefined
   d. Undefined

108. _____ is a subset of a population.
   a. Sample0
   b. Thing
   c. Undefined
   d. Undefined

109. _____ is the production of food, feed, fiber, fuel and other goods by the systematic raizing of plants and animals.
   a. Thing
   b. Agriculture0
   c. Undefined
   d. Undefined

110. _____ is a set, with some particular properties and usually some additional structure, such as the operations of addition or multiplication, for instance.
   a. Thing
   b. Space0
   c. Undefined
   d. Undefined

111. In probability theory, the _____ or universal _____, often denoted S, Ù or U (for "universe"), of an experiment or random trial is the set of all possible outcomes.
   a. Sample space0
   b. Thing
   c. Undefined
   d. Undefined

112. A _____ is a three-dimensional solid object bounded by six square faces, facets, or sides, with three meeting at each vertex.
   a. Thing
   b. Cube0
   c. Undefined
   d. Undefined

113. If the probabilities of simple events are all the same, then they are _____. This occurs in a uniform sample space.
   a. Thing
   b. Equally likely0
   c. Undefined
   d. Undefined

114. In probability theory, _____ are various sets of outcomes (a subset of the sample space) to which a probability is assigned.
   a. Thing
   b. Events0
   c. Undefined
   d. Undefined

## Chapter 7. Sequences, Series, and Combinatorics

115. In physics, _____ is an influence that may cause an object to accelerate. It may be experienced as a lift, a push, or a pull. The actual acceleration of the body is determined by the vector sum of all forces acting on it, known as net _____ or resultant _____.
   a. Thing
   b. Force0
   c. Undefined
   d. Undefined

116. In mathematics, the _____ of a function is the set of all "output" values produced by that function. Given a function $f : A \rightarrow B$, the _____ of $f$, is defined to be the set $\{x \in B : x = f(a) \text{ for some } a \in A\}$.
   a. Thing
   b. Range0
   c. Undefined
   d. Undefined

117. A _____ number is a positive integer which has a positive divisor other than one or itself.
   a. Composite0
   b. Thing
   c. Undefined
   d. Undefined

118. A _____, formed by the composition of one function on another, represents the application of the former to the result of the application of the latter to the argument of the composite.
   a. Thing
   b. Composite function0
   c. Undefined
   d. Undefined

119. _____ element of an element x with respect to a binary operation * with identity element e is an element y such that $x * y = y * x = e$. In particular,
   a. Inverse0
   b. Thing
   c. Undefined
   d. Undefined

120. An _____ is a function which does the reverse of a given function.
   a. Thing
   b. Inverse function0
   c. Undefined
   d. Undefined

121. In mathematics and logic, a _____ proof is a way of showing the truth or falsehood of a given statement by a straightforward combination of established facts, usually existing lemmas and theorems, without making any further assumptions.
   a. Direct0
   b. Thing
   c. Undefined
   d. Undefined

122. _____ is the relationship between two variables, like a ratio in which the two quantities being compared are different units.
   a. Direct variation0
   b. Thing
   c. Undefined
   d. Undefined

123. In mathematics, a _____ number is a number which can be expressed as a ratio of two integers. Non-integer _____ numbers (commonly called fractions) are usually written as the vulgar fraction a / b, where b is not zero.
   a. Rational0
   b. Thing
   c. Undefined
   d. Undefined

## Chapter 7. Sequences, Series, and Combinatorics

124. A _____ is a set of numbers that designate location in a given reference system, such as x,y in a planar _____ system or an x,y,z in a three-dimensional _____ system.
a. Coordinate0  
b. Thing  
c. Undefined  
d. Undefined

125. In mathematics and the mathematical sciences, a _____ is a fixed, but possibly unspecified, value. This is in contrast to a variable, which is not fixed.
a. Thing  
b. Constant0  
c. Undefined  
d. Undefined

126. _____ is a mathematical science pertaining to the collection, analysis, interpretation or explanation, and presentation of data. It is applicable to a wide variety of academic disciplines, from the physical and social sciences to the humanities.
a. Thing  
b. Statistics0  
c. Undefined  
d. Undefined

127. The word _____ comes from the Latin word linearis, which means created by lines.
a. Linear0  
b. Thing  
c. Undefined  
d. Undefined

128. _____, from Latin meaning "to make progress", is defined in two different ways. Pure economic _____ is the increase in wealth that an investor has from making an investment, taking into consideration all costs associated with that investment including the opportunity cost of capital.
a. Thing  
b. Profit0  
c. Undefined  
d. Undefined

# ANSWER KEY

**Chapter 1**

| | | | | | | | | | |
|---|---|---|---|---|---|---|---|---|---|
| 1. b | 2. a | 3. a | 4. a | 5. b | 6. a | 7. a | 8. a | 9. a | 10. a |
| 11. a | 12. a | 13. b | 14. b | 15. a | 16. a | 17. a | 18. a | 19. b | 20. b |
| 21. a | 22. b | 23. b | 24. a | 25. b | 26. a | 27. b | 28. b | 29. b | 30. b |
| 31. a | 32. b | 33. b | 34. b | 35. a | 36. a | 37. b | 38. b | 39. a | 40. b |
| 41. a | 42. b | 43. b | 44. b | 45. b | 46. a | 47. b | 48. a | 49. a | 50. b |
| 51. b | 52. b | 53. a | 54. a | 55. b | 56. b | 57. b | 58. a | 59. b | 60. b |
| 61. a | 62. b | 63. a | 64. a | 65. a | 66. b | 67. a | 68. a | 69. b | 70. a |
| 71. b | 72. a | 73. b | 74. b | 75. a | 76. a | 77. a | 78. b | 79. a | 80. a |
| 81. b | 82. a | 83. a | 84. a | 85. b | 86. b | 87. a | 88. b | 89. b | 90. a |
| 91. a | 92. b | 93. b | 94. b | 95. b | 96. b | 97. b | 98. a | 99. b | 100. a |
| 101. a | 102. b | 103. b | 104. a | 105. b | 106. a | 107. a | 108. b | 109. a | 110. a |
| 111. a | 112. a | 113. a | 114. a | 115. a | 116. b | 117. a | 118. a | 119. b | 120. b |
| 121. b | 122. b | 123. a | | | | | | | |

**Chapter 2**

| | | | | | | | | | |
|---|---|---|---|---|---|---|---|---|---|
| 1. a | 2. a | 3. b | 4. a | 5. a | 6. b | 7. b | 8. a | 9. a | 10. a |
| 11. b | 12. a | 13. b | 14. b | 15. b | 16. a | 17. b | 18. b | 19. b | 20. b |
| 21. a | 22. a | 23. b | 24. b | 25. b | 26. b | 27. a | 28. a | 29. b | 30. a |
| 31. b | 32. a | 33. a | 34. b | 35. b | 36. b | 37. a | 38. a | 39. b | 40. a |
| 41. a | 42. a | 43. a | 44. a | 45. b | 46. b | 47. b | 48. b | 49. b | 50. a |
| 51. a | 52. b | 53. b | 54. a | 55. b | 56. b | 57. a | 58. b | 59. b | 60. a |
| 61. b | 62. a | 63. b | 64. b | 65. b | 66. b | 67. b | 68. b | 69. b | 70. b |
| 71. b | 72. b | 73. b | 74. b | 75. b | 76. b | 77. b | 78. b | 79. b | 80. b |
| 81. a | 82. b | 83. b | 84. b | 85. a | 86. b | 87. a | 88. a | 89. a | 90. b |
| 91. a | 92. a | 93. a | 94. b | 95. a | 96. b | 97. a | 98. b | 99. b | 100. b |
| 101. b | 102. a | 103. b | 104. b | 105. b | 106. b | 107. a | 108. a | 109. b | 110. b |
| 111. b | 112. a | 113. b | 114. a | 115. a | 116. a | 117. b | 118. b | 119. a | 120. a |
| 121. b | 122. a | 123. b | 124. b | 125. b | 126. a | 127. a | 128. a | 129. b | 130. a |
| 131. a | 132. a | 133. a | 134. a | 135. b | 136. a | 137. a | 138. b | 139. b | 140. b |
| 141. a | 142. a | 143. b | 144. b | 145. b | 146. b | 147. a | 148. a | 149. a | 150. b |
| 151. b | 152. a | 153. a | 154. b | 155. a | 156. a | 157. a | 158. b | 159. b | 160. b |
| 161. b | 162. a | 163. a | 164. a | 165. b | 166. a | 167. b | 168. a | 169. a | 170. a |
| 171. b | 172. a | 173. b | 174. a | 175. a | 176. b | 177. a | 178. b | 179. a | 180. a |

## Chapter 3

| | | | | | | | | | |
|---|---|---|---|---|---|---|---|---|---|
| 1. a | 2. b | 3. b | 4. a | 5. b | 6. b | 7. a | 8. b | 9. a | 10. a |
| 11. b | 12. a | 13. b | 14. a | 15. b | 16. b | 17. b | 18. a | 19. b | 20. a |
| 21. b | 22. a | 23. b | 24. a | 25. a | 26. a | 27. b | 28. b | 29. a | 30. b |
| 31. a | 32. b | 33. a | 34. b | 35. a | 36. b | 37. b | 38. a | 39. b | 40. b |
| 41. b | 42. b | 43. b | 44. b | 45. b | 46. b | 47. a | 48. b | 49. a | 50. b |
| 51. b | 52. b | 53. a | 54. b | 55. a | 56. a | 57. a | 58. b | 59. a | 60. a |
| 61. a | 62. b | 63. a | 64. b | 65. a | 66. b | 67. b | 68. a | 69. a | 70. a |
| 71. a | 72. b | 73. b | 74. b | 75. a | 76. a | 77. b | 78. a | 79. b | 80. a |
| 81. b | 82. a | 83. b | 84. a | 85. b | 86. a | 87. a | 88. a | 89. a | 90. a |
| 91. a | 92. b | 93. b | 94. a | 95. a | 96. a | 97. a | 98. a | 99. b | 100. a |
| 101. b | 102. b | 103. a | 104. a | 105. a | 106. b | 107. b | 108. a | 109. a | 110. b |
| 111. a | 112. b | 113. b | 114. a | 115. a | 116. a | 117. a | 118. a | 119. a | 120. a |
| 121. b | 122. b | 123. a | 124. a | 125. a | 126. a | 127. b | 128. b | 129. b | 130. a |
| 131. a | 132. a | 133. b | 134. b | 135. b | 136. a | 137. a | 138. b | 139. a | 140. b |
| 141. b | 142. a | 143. a | 144. b | 145. b | 146. b | 147. a | 148. b | 149. a | 150. b |
| 151. a | | | | | | | | | |

## Chapter 4

| | | | | | | | | | |
|---|---|---|---|---|---|---|---|---|---|
| 1. b | 2. a | 3. b | 4. b | 5. a | 6. b | 7. a | 8. a | 9. b | 10. b |
| 11. a | 12. a | 13. b | 14. a | 15. b | 16. a | 17. a | 18. a | 19. b | 20. a |
| 21. b | 22. b | 23. a | 24. a | 25. b | 26. a | 27. a | 28. a | 29. a | 30. b |
| 31. a | 32. b | 33. b | 34. a | 35. a | 36. b | 37. a | 38. b | 39. b | 40. b |
| 41. b | 42. a | 43. a | 44. a | 45. a | 46. b | 47. b | 48. b | 49. a | 50. a |
| 51. b | 52. a | 53. b | 54. a | 55. b | 56. a | 57. b | 58. b | 59. b | 60. b |
| 61. a | 62. a | 63. b | 64. a | 65. a | 66. a | 67. a | 68. b | 69. b | 70. a |
| 71. a | 72. b | 73. b | 74. b | 75. b | 76. b | 77. b | 78. b | 79. b | 80. a |
| 81. a | 82. a | 83. b | 84. a | 85. b | 86. b | 87. b | 88. a | 89. a | 90. b |
| 91. a | 92. a | 93. a | 94. a | 95. b | 96. a | 97. a | 98. b | 99. a | 100. a |
| 101. a | 102. b | 103. a | 104. a | 105. a | 106. b | 107. a | 108. b | 109. b | 110. a |
| 111. a | 112. a | 113. a | 114. a | 115. a | 116. b | 117. b | 118. a | 119. a | 120. a |
| 121. a | 122. b | 123. b | 124. a | 125. a | 126. b | 127. a | 128. a | 129. a | 130. b |
| 131. b | 132. a | 133. a | 134. b | 135. a | 136. b | 137. a | 138. b | 139. a | 140. b |
| 141. b | 142. a | 143. a | 144. a | 145. b | 146. b | 147. a | 148. b | 149. a | 150. b |
| 151. a | 152. b | 153. a | 154. b | 155. a | 156. b | 157. a | 158. b | 159. b | 160. a |

# ANSWER KEY

**Chapter 5**

| | | | | | | | | | |
|---|---|---|---|---|---|---|---|---|---|
| 1. a | 2. b | 3. b | 4. a | 5. a | 6. a | 7. a | 8. a | 9. a | 10. b |
| 11. a | 12. b | 13. a | 14. a | 15. a | 16. b | 17. b | 18. b | 19. b | 20. b |
| 21. a | 22. a | 23. a | 24. a | 25. a | 26. a | 27. a | 28. a | 29. a | 30. a |
| 31. b | 32. a | 33. b | 34. a | 35. a | 36. b | 37. b | 38. b | 39. a | 40. b |
| 41. b | 42. b | 43. b | 44. a | 45. a | 46. a | 47. b | 48. a | 49. a | 50. a |
| 51. a | 52. a | 53. b | 54. b | 55. a | 56. a | 57. b | 58. b | 59. b | 60. a |
| 61. a | 62. b | 63. b | 64. b | 65. b | 66. a | 67. a | 68. a | 69. a | 70. b |
| 71. b | 72. a | 73. a | 74. a | 75. b | 76. a | 77. a | 78. a | 79. b | 80. a |
| 81. a | 82. a | 83. b | 84. a | 85. b | 86. a | 87. a | 88. a | 89. a | 90. b |
| 91. a | 92. b | 93. a | 94. a | 95. a | 96. a | 97. a | 98. a | 99. a | 100. b |
| 101. b | 102. a | 103. a | 104. b | 105. b | 106. b | 107. b | 108. a | 109. b | 110. b |
| 111. b | 112. b | 113. a | 114. a | 115. a | 116. a | 117. a | 118. a | 119. b | 120. b |
| 121. b | 122. a | 123. b | 124. b | 125. a | 126. b | 127. a | 128. a | 129. b | 130. b |
| 131. a | 132. a | 133. b | 134. a | 135. a | 136. a | 137. a | 138. b | 139. a | 140. a |
| 141. a | 142. b | 143. b | 144. a | 145. b | 146. b | 147. b | 148. a | 149. b | 150. b |
| 151. a | 152. b | 153. b | 154. a | 155. b | 156. b | 157. b | 158. a | 159. a | 160. b |
| 161. b | 162. a | 163. b | 164. b | 165. a | 166. b | 167. a | 168. b | 169. b | 170. b |
| 171. a | 172. a | 173. a | 174. b | 175. a | 176. a | 177. b | 178. a | 179. a | 180. a |
| 181. b | 182. b | 183. a | 184. a | 185. a | 186. a | 187. a | 188. b | 189. a | 190. b |
| 191. b | 192. a | 193. b | 194. a | 195. a | 196. b | 197. b | 198. b | 199. a | 200. a |
| 201. b | 202. a | 203. a | 204. b | 205. b | 206. b | 207. a | 208. a | 209. b | 210. a |
| 211. b | 212. a | 213. a | 214. a | 215. a | 216. a | 217. a | 218. b | 219. b | 220. a |
| 221. a | | | | | | | | | |

**Chapter 6**

| | | | | | | | | | |
|---|---|---|---|---|---|---|---|---|---|
| 1. a | 2. b | 3. a | 4. b | 5. a | 6. b | 7. a | 8. a | 9. b | 10. b |
| 11. b | 12. b | 13. a | 14. a | 15. a | 16. b | 17. b | 18. a | 19. a | 20. a |
| 21. b | 22. a | 23. a | 24. b | 25. a | 26. b | 27. a | 28. b | 29. b | 30. a |
| 31. a | 32. a | 33. b | 34. a | 35. b | 36. a | 37. a | 38. a | 39. b | 40. b |
| 41. b | 42. a | 43. b | 44. a | 45. a | 46. a | 47. a | 48. b | 49. a | 50. b |
| 51. b | 52. b | 53. a | 54. a | 55. a | 56. b | 57. a | 58. b | 59. a | 60. a |
| 61. b | 62. b | 63. b | 64. a | 65. a | 66. a | 67. b | 68. b | 69. a | 70. b |
| 71. b | 72. b | 73. a | 74. b | 75. a | 76. b | 77. b | 78. a | 79. a | 80. b |
| 81. a | 82. b | 83. a | 84. b | 85. a | 86. b | 87. b | 88. b | 89. b | 90. b |
| 91. a | 92. a | 93. b | 94. b | 95. a | 96. b | 97. b | 98. a | | |

**Chapter 7**

| | | | | | | | | | |
|---|---|---|---|---|---|---|---|---|---|
| 1. b | 2. a | 3. a | 4. b | 5. b | 6. b | 7. a | 8. b | 9. a | 10. a |
| 11. b | 12. a | 13. b | 14. a | 15. a | 16. b | 17. b | 18. b | 19. a | 20. a |
| 21. a | 22. a | 23. a | 24. a | 25. b | 26. b | 27. a | 28. a | 29. a | 30. b |
| 31. a | 32. a | 33. a | 34. b | 35. b | 36. a | 37. b | 38. a | 39. a | 40. b |
| 41. b | 42. a | 43. b | 44. a | 45. a | 46. b | 47. a | 48. a | 49. a | 50. a |
| 51. b | 52. b | 53. a | 54. b | 55. b | 56. b | 57. b | 58. b | 59. b | 60. b |
| 61. a | 62. a | 63. b | 64. b | 65. a | 66. b | 67. a | 68. b | 69. a | 70. b |
| 71. b | 72. a | 73. a | 74. b | 75. b | 76. a | 77. b | 78. a | 79. b | 80. a |
| 81. b | 82. a | 83. a | 84. a | 85. b | 86. a | 87. a | 88. a | 89. b | 90. b |
| 91. a | 92. b | 93. a | 94. a | 95. a | 96. b | 97. b | 98. a | 99. b | 100. b |
| 101. a | 102. b | 103. a | 104. a | 105. b | 106. b | 107. b | 108. a | 109. b | 110. b |
| 111. a | 112. b | 113. b | 114. b | 115. b | 116. b | 117. a | 118. b | 119. a | 120. b |
| 121. a | 122. a | 123. a | 124. a | 125. b | 126. b | 127. a | 128. b | | |

www.ingramcontent.com/pod-product-compliance
Lightning Source LLC
Chambersburg PA
CBHW082048230426
43670CB00016B/2822